Where the Lysanders were . . .

The story of Sawbridgeworth's airfields

Paul A. Doyle

Forward Airfield Research Publishing ⟫

First published in 1995 by
Forward Airfield Research Publishing
2 Carmelo Court, Beamish Close
North Weald, Essex CM16 6UA
England

Original typesetting by West 4 Printers Ltd.
8 Essex Place, London W4 5UT

Reprinted 1996, 1997, 2000, 2006, 2010, 2021

Republished (with amendments) in 2010 by
Forward Airfield Research Publishing
1 Stirling Cottages, Hurdles Way,
Duxford, Cambridgeshire CB22 4AE
England

Reset in 2010 by
Streets Printers
15 Royston Road, Baldock
Hertfordshire SG7 6NW
Reprinted in 2010 by Xerox Ltd

Reprinted in 2021 by the Sawbridgeworth Local History Society
Printed by C Z Design & Print, Unit 3, Southmill Trading Centre,
Bishop's Stortford, Hertfordshire CM23 3DY

ISBN 0 9525624 0 5

Front cover photograph:
Flight Lieutenant F M 'Barney' Benito taxying Lysander L4687, one of the
66 Mk 1 produced and the first to be delivered to 2 (AC) Squadron in 1938.

The stub wing and rear fuselage bomb racks are empty and the message
pickup hook is in the retracted position, whilst flaps are partially down and
the leading edge slats and engine cooling gills are open. Wheel covers were
routinely removed to prevent mud from rough fields clogging the wheels.

Frank Benito served with 2 {AC) Squadron until leaving in 1935 to run
a public house in Everleigh, Wiltshire, but rejoined in 1938.

Photo via 2 (AC) Squadron library

Contents

Acknowledgements

Without my persistent pestering of the following this book would not have been written, therefore I give grateful thanks for the assistance and time freely given by:

SAWBRIDGEWORTH

Ron Brittain, Terry Bruce (Blounts Farm), Gina Frost, John and Mrs Hills (managers, The Memorial Hall), Julius Holder, George Jackson (ex-publican, Allens Green), Peter and Pat Kirby (United Services Club), David Morris and family (Blounts and Shingle Hall Farms), Sid and Mrs Napier (ex 2 Sqn), Terry Oatham (USC), Eric Rogers and staff (Town Council), John Sapsford, Keith Taylor (Tharbies), Rob and Gwen Trundle (publicans, Allens Green), Doreen and Wally Wright (Bishops Stortford Local Historical Society)

GREEN TYE

Geoff Ashwell (Warren Farm), Derek Bird, Aubrey Flowers, Chris and Mrs Glyn (ex 5 AIL Section)

THORLEY

The late Doris Barker, Jack and Mrs Bird, Kenneth Cook, Liz Eldred (shepherdess)

ALSO:

Murray Adams (ex 80 Sqn, Australia), Ron Bayford (Little Hallingbury), Ken Bell (ex The RAFR, Worcester), Philip Birtles (Stevenage) Dr Ron Blake (Airfield Research Group), Bill Bowker (ex Bowker Air Services, Hitchin), Fl Lt Roger Brookwick (No 2 (AC) Squadron, Marham), Colin Brown (En-tout-cas, Leicester), Peter Brown (ex 1096 ATC Sqn, Bishops Stortford), John Burke (John Burke Associates, Romford), Brandon Chapman (ATC/NATS, Stansted Airport), Denis Clarke (ex 170 and 268 Sqns, Hampshire), Doug Coxhead (ex 182 Sqn, Sussex), Graham Crisp (ARG), Reg Davey (RAFA, Totteridge), Steven Day (Little Hadham), Ken Delve (ex 2 Sqn, Editor – *Flypast* Magazine), Denis Downes (ex 2 Sqn, Leicester), Ken Ellis (BAPC, Rutland), Col Eustace Elwes (ex 2 Sqn AILO, Norfolk), Len Eve (ex Bursteads, Bishops Stortford), Michael Fahie (Western Australia), Paul Fahie (Salisbury), Eric Faircloth (Albury), Ken Fisher (ex 2 and 63 Sqns, Exmouth), the Fleet Air Arm Museum, Frank Foreman (ex W & C French, N Yorks), Ken Fossey (ex 2 Sqn, Lancashire), Paul Francis, Roger Freeman, John Hamlin and Brian Martin (ARG), Ray Funnel and Clive Richards (RAF Museum), the Glyn family (Albury), Jim Godden (ex 2nd TAF, Derby), Ted Gould (Albury), Dennis Gumming (ex 2 Sqn, Feltham), Cdr Ronnie Hay (ex 809 FAA, Wiltshire), staff at Hertford CRO, *Herts & Essex Observer* newspapers, Hertford Fire and Rescue Service, Peter Hood and staff (Home Office), Jack Jarvis (ex 35 Wing Signals Section, West Lothian), Maurice Lissner (ex 268 Sqn, Dulwich), Peter Long (ex Fisons and Fieldspray, Colchester), Albert Mann (ex 63 and 268 Sqns, Dumfries-shire), Peter Mariner (ex 809 FAA, Dorset), Les Marriott (ex 2 Sqn, Scunthorpe), C J Mason (ex 2 Sqn, Clwyd), Stuart McKay (DH Moth Club, Berkhamsted), Leslie R Miller (Hoddesdon), J G 'Hans' Onderwater (2 Sqn historian, The Netherlands), Mike Packham (Mosquito Aircraft Museum, Panshanger), Jim Palmer (ex 268 Sqn AILO, Hampshire), Norman Pattison (ex 2 Sqn, Somersham), Gerald Percival (ex 2 Sqn, Bury St Edmunds), Fred Pond (ex 2 Sqn, South London), Michael Ridley-Martin (ex 170 Sqn, South Devon), Harry Roberts (HMP), Royal Air Force Personnel Management Centre (Gloucester), Peter Smith (ex Fisons, Bermondsey), Ray C Sturtivant (FAA/military aviation historian, St Albans), Jim Syratt (170 Sqn Association, Leicester), Martin and Mrs Thompson (ex The RAFR, RAF Regiment Museum, Honington), Ernest Tomlinson (ex RAF Chigwell, Preston), Peter Tonkin (ex 2 Sqn, Great Canfield), Donna Walsh (AHRG/MoD), past and present members of Ware Fire Brigade, Sue Waugh (Patmore Hall Farm, Albury), Alan Webb (ex RAF Hornchurch, Gidea Park), Robert Weighill (ex 2 Sqn, Halton), David Wiles (ex 53 MFH, Luton), George Wilson (ex 80 Sqn, Lincoln) and Brian Woods (Theydon Bois).

Special thanks are extended to Geoff Ashwell, John Burke (my 1994 PR pilot), Ken Delve, David Morris, Sid Napier, Sawbridgeworth Town Council, Rob Trundle and all at 2 (AC) Squadron (Marham) – plus those inadvertently forgotten . . .

Grateful thanks are also due to Eric Buckmaster at Sawbridgeworth Town Council, and Xerox Ltd for assisting with the 2010 reprint.

Introduction

This is the story of a flying site in Hertfordshire that has been generally forgotten due to its having been mentioned briefly by so few writers, whether they be official researchers, magazine columnists or compilers of airfield histories in any form. Quite often referred to merely as 'one of those muddy little fields that RAF Lysanders used to fly out of in the Second World War' it has never been expanded upon to tell the full story of what went on during the six stages of development of the flying sites situated on those same muddy little fields in between the three main farmsteads mentioned in this book.

It is possible that because the early days were not well documented, or that the work of Army Co-operation Squadrons did not achieve the same glamour as did the 'fighter boys' from Biggin Hill or Hornchurch, or that the activities of SOE were not widely publicised (for obvious reasons), or that no-one remembers what MFHs or CAEUs did has caused Sawbridgeworth to slip through time unnoticed. Another more pertinent fact is that locals living in the nearby hamlets or farms at High Wych, Trims Green or Shingle Hall always considered the airfield they lived near to be their own, therefore usage of the local name over many years meant that further generations never knew it as RAF Sawbridgeworth, as it became officially known.

It is hoped that this account will at last put the records straight for Sawbridgeworth, an airfield site used from the early days of flying until it was finally forced upon the military powers in the Second World War, mainly by one squadron which returned time after time to pioneer new techniques and equipment on those muddy little fields where the Lysanders were . . .

Paul A Doyle
North Weald 1995

To my children,

for whom I am deeply grateful

With the locals clustered round, the Farman type biplane sits in the field near the 'Dusty Miller' public house, Gilston, on 26 June 1912.

Early Beginnings

The advent of the aeroplane, initially as a fighting machine, was viewed with awe by the majority of the general public not generally able to get close enough to one to be able to form their own opinions. This was even more so for country folk, many of whom were not able to keep in touch with developments in this field as reported by the news media of the day.

For the inhabitants of Pye Corner, two miles south of Sawbridgeworth, this changed on 26 June 1912 when Lewis Turner, chief pilot for the Grahame-White Aviation Company at Hendon Aerodrome force-landed a Farman biplane near the Dusty Miller public house. A stir was created, villages flocked to it, and Gilston school was closed for pupils to see this marvel of the new age. Later that day it took off but crashed into trees, and the recovery lorry from Hendon collected the fragile craft and even after it had been long gone the event was a topic of conversation for some time.

The First World War

With the start of the First World War the employment of the aeroplane, in its new habitat of countrywide flying grounds, meant that ordinary people began to see more and more of it. In April 1916 the Home Defence detachments at Suttons and Hainault Farms, Essex, were merged to form 39 Squadron RFC and as such was sent to North Weald Bassett, a 1st Class flight station in Eastern Command near Epping, where it operated as a full unit. Its main role was the defence of London against the high-altitude German bombers and airships, and immediately on its arrival there searches were made northwards to establish further landing fields for the squadron.

Such fields, designated as night landing grounds and positioned at set distances from the flight station and each other, were only intended to enable aircraft experiencing an engine failure or loss of bearings during the course of a night patrol to make a safe landing if they could not reach their home base. Whilst 39 Squadron had a number of sites already allocated to it (two 1st, two 2nd and six 3rd Class) it was agreed to provide yet more and three locations were surveyed in the area of Sawbridgeworth. Aviation was being born in this corner of Hertfordshire.

The largest of these, at 56 acres, was level ground with very good approaches from two directions and situated at the junction of West and Cambridge Roads. However after the land had been acquired it was apparent that the site was far too close to the town itself for safe operation and it was returned to its owners.

The smallest site, just to the north-east of Tharbies Farm, also had good approaches but with its usable area being only 24 acres and topographically unsuitable by virtue of it being on top of rising ground it too was not pursued.

Finally a site to the west of Shingle Hall was acquired which had an area of only 31 acres but was level, had the benefit of good approaches in all directions and was also clear of populated areas. In the ownership of Mr Lukies, a public road ran along the northern boundary. This made for easy access whilst its location, two and a half miles from the main line railway station at Sawbridgeworth, enhanced its selection and use as a practical landing site.

The site was fully established by the end of April and achieved the status of a 2nd Class night landing ground in 6th Brigade serving 39 Squadron of the 49th Wing, Midland Area. The landing area measured 450 yds x 300 yds and occupied one field to the west of the Hall, south of Much Hadham Road at grid reference TL 465175. It had only a windsock and hut for pyrotechnics but, whilst no aircraft hangarage or repair facilities were provided, the luxury of the telephone had not been missed, for by day the LG could be reached on Sawbridgeworth 1 and by night on Sawbridgeworth 17.

When in operation at night the site was manned by civilians recruited locally, with an RFC officer in over-all charge, whose job was to lay out according to wind direction an L-shaped pattern of 'Money' flares with the long leg pointing down-wind. The flares comprised an asbestos wick soaked in paraffin inside a wire cage and burnt at the rate of one and a quarter gallons per hour. This

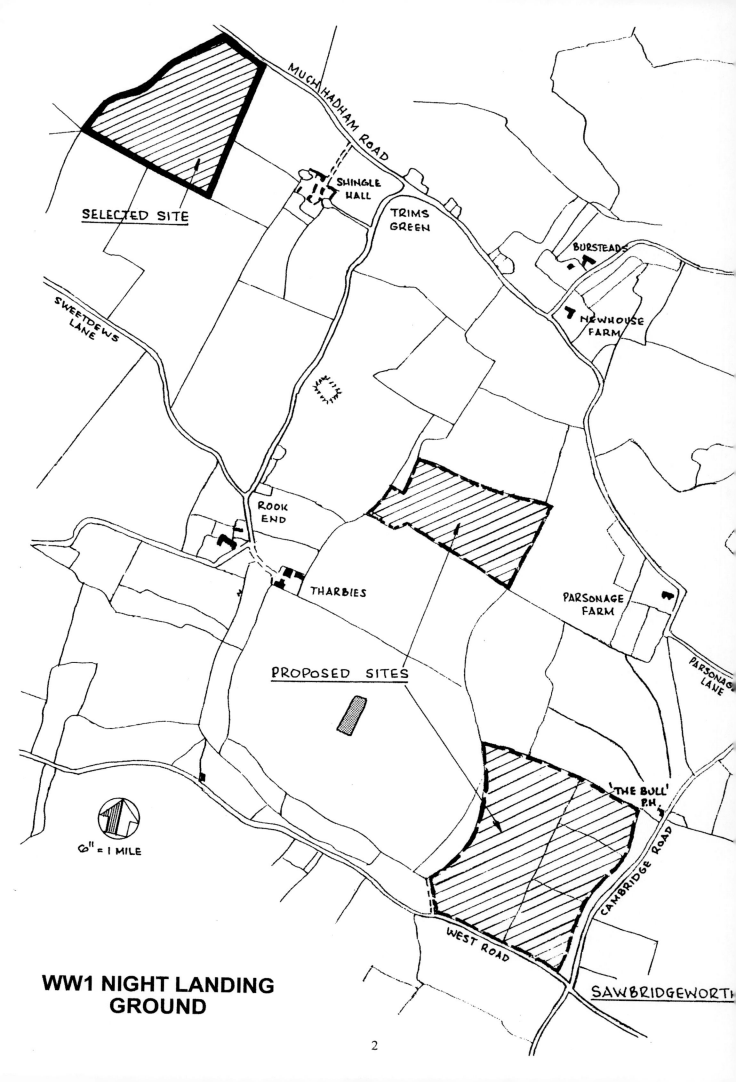

SELECTED SITE

MUCH HADHAM ROAD

SHINGLE HALL

TRIMS GREEN

BURSTEADS

NEWHOUSE FARM

SWEETDEWS LANE

ROOK END

THARBIES

PARSONAGE FARM

PARSONAGE LANE

PROPOSED SITES

6" = 1 MILE

'THE BULL' P.H.

CAMBRIDGE ROAD

WEST ROAD

SAWBRIDGEWORTH

WW1 NIGHT LANDING GROUND

2

portable flarepath, placed on the upwind boundary each night the site was in operation and lit when an aeroplane was overhead, proved extremely effective in showing through mist and fog at this period in time – the same layout proving effective when used in practices for another purpose on the same site some 25 years later, but that is covered in another chapter.

Accommodation on site was limited to a felt-covered wooden hut or the odd tent as a bad weather shelter for the men and by the very nature of the reason for the existence of the landing ground any aeroplane using it did not stay long before returning to its home station. One example noted by Len Eve of Bursteads was a Bristol Fighter with the inscription 'Zanzibar the 8th' which, after taxi-ing out for take-off one morning, failed to get airborne and went through the hedge on the east side.

The second recorded out-landing occurred on 14 September 1917 when an unknown RFC machine came down at Tednambury, two fields away from Spellbrook CE village school. This time no holiday was given but five of the pupils played truant to walk across the muddy fields to see the sight. When their absence was noticed the teacher had to come to get the absconders.

The incident was reported only briefly in the local press, for heavy censorship was still in force, and newspapers were more concerned with the world-wide conflict being carried out on a much larger scale.

The landing ground continued in use at least until 16 November 1918, when it was still 'on the books' of North Weald Bassett and marked as an LG on service maps, but was de-requisitioned after this time and the site returned to agriculture.

The Mid-war Years

After lying dormant to flying for some ten years, whilst acceding to the needs of farming, wings returned to the site in 1928 when an embryonic gliding club was formed at Shingle Hall, the farm still owned and worked by Mr Lukies who now lived at Blounts Farm. It is not known who the members were except that they were locals, how many attempted this daring new sport, or even what types of glider were used, but local steam plough driver Julius Holder (having been engaged to lay mole drains across the farm in 1926) can recall launches being made from the second meadow to the west of Shingle Hall using initially a hand winch. When this ceased to work, or ran out of volunteers to power it, an old Bentley car was pressed into service as a launch vehicle to provide what are now known in gliding circles as 'straight auto-tows' across the grassy surface.

Certainly the club, for want of a better description, existed for no more than a year as the Hertfordshire Mercury noted in 1932 that ploughing matches had been held in the area for three years, no mention being made then of any aerial activity associated with the Shingle Hall site.

A year later all this was to change, and Shingle Hall was once again host to those magnificent men and their flying machines. Flushed with the success of Sir Alan Cobham's National Aviation Days, organised to operate on a daily basis from 1932-35 all over England, a rival organisation was set up early in 1933 by Barker, Cobham's own secretary, who had left him at the end of the 1932 season. Calling itself the British Hospitals Air Pageant it ran the flying display side on a similar vein to Cobham but its ulterior motives were somewhat different.

For this new venture to succeed in the wake of Cobham's success it was necessary for a famous name to be associated with it, accordingly Barker selected C W A Scott to head it. Scott was already well known in the field of aviation but would become even more so in 1934 as one half of the team that took the DH88 Comet Racer to victory in the England-Australia air race. The new venture duly commenced operations using as its theme the financial support for hospitals local to the area in which the daily displays were staged. However many deceptive claims were made about the extent to which the hospitals would actually benefit from it. Being well before the days of the National Health Service it seemed to be a charitable institution but in fact merely exploited the gullibility of the charity-minded.

Because Cobham visited such nearby locations as Enfield on 15-16 May 1932 and Hertford on 20

April 1933, and his advertising machine was well-tuned to attract the public eye in many ways including the use of newspapers and on posters, most of the public tended to think of any form of travelling flying circus as being his. This was however not so when the BHAP circus came to town, or to be more precise the Spellbrook Flying Ground at Shingle Hall on Wednesday, 17 May 1933.

As part of the advertising machine, and spurred on by the spirit of the event, the *Herts and Essex Observer* got into the swing of things by billing it as the 'Great Air Pageant' in its 22 April issue and, on 6 May, offered 15 free flights for readers to take when the Air Pageant visited. The winners were duly posted in the 13 May issue and it is noted that six were from Sawbridgeworth; however it is sad to report that not one of the 15 is around today to recall their experiences during the flight.

A further part of the pre-display advertising was the distribution to local schools of a small leaflet, compiled by Charles Scott, intended to help children understand the basic principles of flight. This took the form of a simple but entertaining flying lesson and was an incitement to 500 or so children to attend the Pageant and see the lesson demonstrated by means of a 'radio-controlled' aeroplane. This practical display was intended to reach the younger more easily-impressed end of the market, who were also given free balloons (a common ploy with many generations) as a bonus when they arrived.

The Observer reported the event in the 20 May issue with a full-page spread including photographs. The text ran:

"The first spin with a Drone machine performed in public was seen at the British Hospitals Air Pageant, given at the flying ground, Spelbrook (sic) on Wednesday in aid of Bishops Stortford Hospital. This feat was performed by Mr C J Longmore – the only man who has looped the loop in a glider – in a BAC Drone aeroplane fitted with a 6 h.p motorcycle engine, realistically painted to represent a dragon by that well-known artist, Mr William Heath Robinson."

(He was later to be associated with complex inventions of a ramshackle nature, and his name subsequently becaming a household attribute to any home-made gadget, especially if it did not function to perfection.)

It continued :

"The Pageant, which is the largest that has ever visited Bishops Stortford, was well worth a visit and was excellently organised. Under the leadership of Capt Charles W A Scott, AFC, who holds the record of 8 days 20 hours for the England to Australia flight, made in April last year, the pilots were: Miss Pauline Gower (with her ground engineer Miss Dorothy Norman Spicer), the Hon Mrs Victor Bruce, FRGS, Fl Lt J B W Pugh, AFC, Capt P Phillips, DFC, Capt R H McIntosh, Capt W A Rollason, Capt E B Fielden, Mr T W J Nash, AFM, Mr W H E Drury, Mr L Anderson, Mr E W Bonnar, Mr John K Morton, Fl Lt Hill, Mr C J Longmore, Capt Jordan and others. The first man to fly the Atlantic from East to West, Col J Fitzmaurice, acted as compere. It is doubtful if a gathering of more famous and representative pilots could be formed."

(Some names are worthy of note, Mesdames Gower, Spicer and Bruce became ATA ferry pilots in WW2, whilst Fielden rose to command the Kings Flight before transferring to Special Operations work.)

The Pageant was opened by Admiral M F Sueter, MP for the Division, with his daughter in attendance. Sueter had been one of the 'founding fathers' of the Naval Air Service in 1909 and reference was made to this in his opening speech. By the time he left he had worked it up to a total of 1000 officers and machines, such was his interest in the flying side of the Service. Admiral Sueter then went on to thank the promoters for inviting him down, he having been described in a recent copy of *Aeroplane* as the father of Naval Aviation, and referred to the fact that England now held the long distance, and until recently the speed record. He closed by speaking of the need for hospitals and the particular work they did for the common good.

Col Fitzmaurice, the compere, then explained that the object of the Pageant was to help the hospitals in the current economic climate. It was stated that the Pageant hoped to hand over at least £100,000

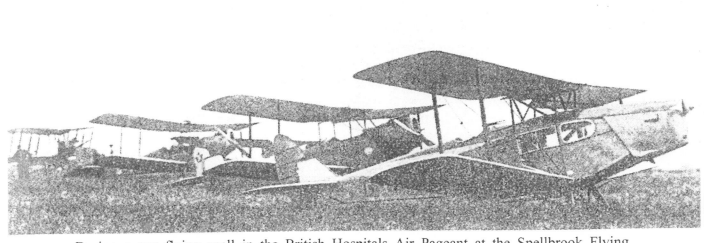

During a non-flying spell in the British Hospitals Air Pageant at the Spellbrook Flying Ground on 17 May 1933 the DH Fox Moth G-ACCF is parked in front of Gipsy Moths G-ABKK and 'BVY and Avro 504N G-EBVY, with an unidentified type behind. Unlike the Gipsy Major engines mounted inverted in the Tiger and Fox Moth variants, which have left-hand tractor propellors stopping at the "five past seven" position, the Gipsy 1 in the Gipsy Moth is mounted "the right way up" with right-hand tractor and stops at the "five to five" position. *Herts and Essex Observer photo via Wally Wright*

Miss Pauline Gower in front of DH Gipsy Moth G-ABKK which she used during the British Hospitals Air Pageant at Spellbrook Flying Ground. An experienced pilot, she later commanded No 1 Ferry Pilot Pool of the Air Transport Auxiliary during the Second World War when she delivered new aircraft varying in size between a Tiger Moth to a Lancaster to operational squadrons. *Photo via Michael and Paul Fahie*

The Hawker Hectors of 13 Squadron RAF picketed and covered for the night in August 1937 next to Newsett. Inside the fence are stocks of aviation fuel with the refuelling bowser behind.

Geoff Ashwell photo

The tented camp site west of Mathams Wood, which can be seen in the background. Although temporary the amount of accommodation required for the 1937 manoeuvres was extensive.

Geoff Ashwell photo

in total to local hospitals, of which £20,000 would be realised in 1933, or so their Public Relations manager had intimated. As a result of the Pageant the Bishops Stortford hospital would receive 10% of the gross gate receipts, about £30-worth of flight tickets, 33% of the programme sales and the gross receipts on the sale of model aircraft and flying books. It was further added that, when the campaign was wound up, all the monies remaining after 5% for management had been deducted would be given to the British Hospitals Association for distribution to hospitals.

The proceedings started with a grand parade and flypast of all the participating machines, before the full programme commenced. This included advanced (for that time) aerobatics, formation flying, wireless-controlled flight and crazy flying. Speciality events were a parachute descent by Fl Lt Hill, who landed in the public enclosure, handkerchief pick-ups by the wingtip of Fl Lt Pugh's aircraft and an air race which was won by Capt Scott in a Fox Moth. The most daring stunt was a wing-walking display atop an Avro 504N by Mr Harry Willis, who not only walked between the wings but balanced himself on the top wing and, with only the merest of handgrips, stayed in this position when the aircraft landed.

There were 15 machines in the Pageant, these included various Avros and Gipsy Moths, a Spartan Cruiser, Fox Moth, Desoutter, Miles Satyr, Fairey Fox and the Drone. The DH84 Dragon, capable of seating 10, took up passengers whilst others were able to experience aerobatics in the capable hands of Capt Phillips.

An *Observer* reporter was taken up by Capt McIntosh in Capt Scott's aircraft to fly over Bishops Stortford. His report must be typical of the impressions many got of their first flight, and reads:

"After getting over that uneasy feeling, often experienced when the machine leaves the ground, that there is nothing under one, the passenger begins to look around. The landing ground was left behind and very soon Thorley Church and the houses around were beneath us, looking exactly like a scale model. Over the green fields we flew until we came to Bishops Stortford where all the well-known landmarks – St Michaels Church, the Corn Exchange, North and South Streets – could easily be discerned. As the machine turned, the writer had a glimpse of the river. Then back to Spelbrook, where a perfect landing was made. A curious thing is that although the speed of the machine is high according to land standards, no sensation of speed is felt."

So ends the reporting of the spectacular BHAP event at Spellbrook by the *Herts and Essex Observer*. Whilst the public attendance was slow to build up initially there were more present towards the afternoon, when many took passenger rides. These cost 5/– (25p) for a circuit of Shingle Hall and Thorley or 7/6d (37½p) if the passenger wanted to go as far as Bishops Stortford itself. For many it was their first chance to see their area from the air, something that was not readily available in those early days of 'social' flying.

The next use for the Shingle Hall site was as an RAF emergency landing ground. *The Air Pilot Supplement* of December 1934 stated that mobile beacons were established at various aerodromes and ELGs, which were to be used occasionally for RAF operational purposes only but were not shown on aviation maps. A list of such places included the reference to:

'Sawbridgeworth – 51° 50' 00" N, 00° 07' 30" E. Code SE'

These co-ordinates place the beacon at the southern edge of the First World War NLG, and explain the presence of the beacon frame noted by Julius Holder which sat in the field corner, 100 yards from the rear drive to Shingle Hall, until it succombed to nature.

The Pre-war Advanced Landing Ground

1937 was the next time that aircraft engines were heard around Sawbridgeworth. In order to provide the RAF with 'on the job' training for the squadrons in 22 Group, Army Co-operation Command, a landing ground was established to the north of the Much Hadham road, south of Newsett and west

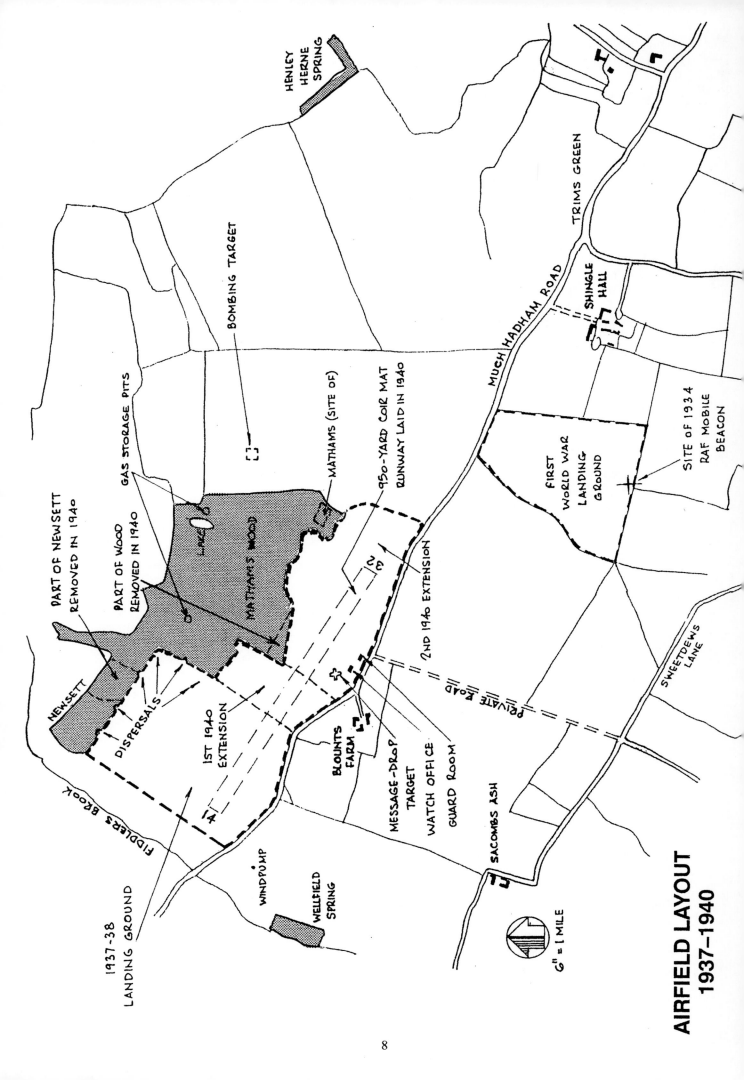

AIRFIELD LAYOUT
1937–1940

6" = 1 MILE

HENLEY HERNE SPRING

TRIMS GREEN

MUCH HADHAM ROAD

SHINGLE HALL

SITE OF 1934 RAF MOBILE BEACON

BOMBING TARGET

FIRST WORLD WAR LANDING GROUND

MATHAMS (SITE OF)

950-YARD COIR MAT RUNWAY LAID IN 1940

SWEETDEWS LANE

GAS STORAGE PITS

PART OF NEWSETT REMOVED IN 1940

PART OF WOOD REMOVED IN 1940

MATHAMS WOOD

32

2ND 1940 EXTENSION

PRIVATE ROAD

NEWSETT

DISPERSALS

1ST 1940 EXTENSION

14

BLOUNTS FARM

MESSAGE-DROP TARGET

WATCH OFFICE

GUARD ROOM

SACOMBS ASH

1937-38 LANDING GROUND

FIDDLERS BROOK

WINDPUMP

WELLFIELD SPRING

8

of Mathams Wood. The 43-acre grass site, situated at map reference TL 456185 (military reference L906365, Sheet 96) and known as Mathams Wood ALG, was used intermittently by Hawker Audax and Hector aircraft from August 1937 until the outbreak of World War Two, with only one aircraft incident recorded in that two-year period. The aircraft park commenced near to Fiddlers Brook on the western boundary and took up the full length of Newsett in order to accommodate a whole squadron, whilst the landing area extended nearly to Blounts Farm entrance. Fuel was normally supplied by bowser, kept on site within the fenced compound which also enclosed the aircraft, but further stocks of standard 2 x 2 gallon packs were also situated at each end of the aircraft park.

In the years up to 1939 only the aircraft park was fenced off, therefore, with the low field boundary fences and hedges, landings took place into wind according to windsock direction. The sole aircraft incident occurred on 13 August 1937 when a 13 Squadron Hector, K8096, was returning to the LG after a close reconnaissance practice. In landing too fast the pilot had no chance to correct swing and the starboard lower wingtip caught the ground, causing slight damage, but both crew members were unhurt. The aircraft was repaired and later served with No 1 School of Army Co-operation until 8 September 1941 when it crashed on Red Pike in the Lake District, killing both crew. The remains are still there today and as such is the only Hawker Hector left in the UK, albeit in hardly presentable condition.

With only ever one squadron at a time on detachment to Mathams Wood there was no need for any permanent buildings to be erected, the wooden hut serving as both watch office and pyrotechnics store being positioned near the Much Hadham road close to an existing footpath which crossed the landing ground from north to south.

Accommodation for all ranks on site was under canvas with the camp area to the west of Mathams Wood itself, and being peace-time no compulsory requisition powers were in force therefore the comforts and delights of nearby Warren and Blounts Farms were not able to be sampled – yet.

The Second World War

The practice of using the field for exercises such as manoeuvres with HQ Command at Aldershot, in addition to other well-established airfields or LGs, continued until war with Germany was declared in September 1939. At this time all Army Co-operation squadrons were ordered to their war stations in southern England before being detached where required to serve the British Expeditionary Force in France and the Low Countries. When the BEF retreated from France in May 1940 the AC squadrons were left to their own devices as to how they got back to their re-assembly airfields in England. No 2 (AC) Squadron, then in 22 Group but operating with 71 Wing, fled Bethune to arrive piecemeal at Lympne, Kent, was re-assembled at nearby Bekesbourne and finally sent to Hatfield in Hertfordshire on 8 June.

Upon arrival at Hatfield an immediate conflict flared up between the RAF and the Ministry of Aircraft Production, the latter claiming that a mass Lysander presence, along with the extra wireless traffic they would create, would attract unwanted enemy attention to the de Havilland aircraft factory already there. The RAF agreed to move out but, to save face, kept one flight of the squadron at Hatfield whilst detaching the other two away on a rotational basis to a nearby convenient landing ground. It had to use a LG, rather than an airfield, as there was no space available on any local airfield at that time to absorb a whole Lysander squadron.

Initially Oakleys Field on Albury Hall Estate, and Farnham Green, both north of Little Hadham were used between 8–15 June but whilst they had served as LGs for detached flights they were both in heavily wooded areas and it was apparent that something larger was required to take a greater number of aircraft.

W/C A J W Geddes, CO of 2 (AC) Squadron, carried out an aerial recce of Mathams Wood ALG which, at 320' AMSL, had been found suitable when previously used by Army Co-operation squadrons. He decided that a more useful landing area could be made if the existing grass-surfaced

ALG was extended into the field to the east so, after getting permission from Mr Lukies at Blounts Farm, Geddes had Royal Engineers from 11 Corps remove the hedge, fill in the ditch and consolidate the area, thereby increasing the ALG size to 54 acres straight away.

Parking stands for the Lysanders were formed by levelling ground at intervals along the south side of Newsett, and around the west and south edges of Mathams Wood, with the aircraft being parked tail-first in clearings under the trees to give some degree of cover from the air. Tailwheels were carried on 'bridges' over the ditch which ran around the edge of the wood.

Mathams Wood Advanced Landing Ground

The ALG re-opened on 15 June when the Flight Offices of 2 (AC) Squadron were duly established at Blounts Farm under Flight Lieutenant Edinger. The two flights at Mathams Wood (as it was still known) were to be relieved in turn by the one remaining at Hatfield; however on the day following the setting-up the weather was so bad that all three flights stayed at Hatfield where short field landing practices were carried out instead. Notwithstanding this, the 7th Hampshires commenced guarding the LG on 18 June and on 26 June the CO, W/C Geddes, arrived for the purpose of arranging a local range for air firing purposes. No records are however available to substantiate his findings in this respect although the ranges at Dengie Flats were available (which spawned the need for Bradwell airfield) as well as off-shore firing at Clacton-on-Sea, West Mersea and The Wash.

The need to complete outstanding photo sorties of Western France meant that the squadron worked hard in June and July, as was evident by overdue returns to base resulting in Lysanders force-landing in Sudbury on 19 June, Doddinghurst the next day and Romford on 4 July. After this last occasion, when the pilot stated that he could not see the LG due to its being too well hidden by surrounding features, attempts were made to provide better facilities.

Following a landing accident on 11 July involving a Lysander in gusty conditions a gap was cut in Newsett Wood to make approaches from the north easier, and the LG extended to the east along the south side of the wood as far as the remains of Mathams, a medieval manor house now marked only by a three-quarter acre moat. This further increased the area to 77 acres and, to provide an all-weather surface, the Harlow Works Repair Depot began the laying of a coir mat runway overlaid with Sommerfeld track to a single NW-SE run of just over 950 yards on headings of 14/32. To give the necessary clearance zone for flying off this run part of the south-west corner of Mathams Wood was removed. These works lasted until October, and whilst in progress flights were detached to Teversham for Tac/R duties with the HQ of 2nd Army Corps, although they frequently alternated between Cambridge and Mathams Wood for gas bombing practices when squadron personnel wore respirators during such periods. One such occasion on 17 August involved some 17 Tiger Moths from 6 EFTS making low-level attacks on the ALG, whilst the whole of 21 August consisted of intermittent practice alerts.

Anti-aircraft defence up to this time consisted of a sole multiple Lewis gun set up on the edge of the LG, near the end of the private track which ran south to Allens Green, and manned by Army personnel. The windsock was here also, along with huts for guard room, watch office, fire engine and ambulance, plus a few tents for airmen placed amongst the chestnut trees on the edge of the field just opposite Blounts Farm. Further defence forces did not appear until September when a Ground Gunners Flight of the Royal Air Force arrived as a defence unit to ring the new perimeter with barbed wire dannerts and position further sand-bagged Lewis gun emplacements at strategic points.

In October the Army provided further AA weapons in the form of 20mm Hispano cannon on ground mountings, but at this time a 'no fire' order was in force, in order to save ammunition for whatever fight was to come. Needless to say, the gunners had itchy trigger fingers and did loose off some rounds at raiders passing temptingly within range. A general reprimand was issued and, after telephones were installed in the gunpits, when low-flying raiders passed on other occasions the guns stayed silent. So did the field telephones.

Hawker Hector K9719 of 2 (AC) Squadron running its massive Napier Dagger engine with both crew members on board (who stole the spinner cap?). Hectors entered service in 1937 as successor to the Hawker Audax, but was only 17 mph faster at 6,500 feet which was not exactly the best height for Army Co-operation work.

Photo via 2 (AC) Sqn library

Great Hyde Hall, once the 2 (AC) Squadron and Station Headquarters as well as home to 211 MU, is now self-contained flats.

The rear of Blounts Farm, which served as the Photographic Section for Air Intelligence Liaison operations. In the background is the main farmhouse, used as squadron HQ, whilst on the left can just be seen one of the barns utilised as a station theatre.

On 23 October the 7th Hampshires handed over responsibility for perimeter defence to the 10th Essex (Holding Battalion), in the meantime road blocks for both pedestrian and traffic control were set up west of Blounts Farm and east of Shingle Hall. Both on the Much Hadham Road these were manned by Local Defence Volunteers (the Home Guard) and added to by a further control down the private road when land in that area was acquired. A petrol store was sited next to the westerly road block with aircraft ordnance stored within the tree canopy of Mathams Wood itself. This also afforded the opportunity to position two concrete pits for storing mustard gas and other noxious substances at its northern extremity.

In August 1940 a Boulton-Paul Defiant was received by 2 (AC) Squadron for trials to see if the type was of any use in Army Co-operation work but after being on the unit strength for only three months and tested personally by Geddes at Sawbridgeworth and Cambridge the verdict was that, for the present at least, the Lysander ideally suited the task in hand. Three Fairey Battles received between November 1941 and May 1943 were similarly dismissed for AC work fairly quickly; however they remained until late in 1943 mainly for use as squadron 'hacks' and were frequently loaned to other units on the station for that very purpose.

On 7 September 1940 2 (AC) Squadron, as well as most of the other units in Southern England, nearly went into action when an invasion scare was started. Emanating from coastal patrols the alarm was passed up the chain of command and the codeword 'Cromwell' sent out by teleprinter over the whole of the Southern Area, such that by 2045 that evening all squadrons were on alert for action. A second 'Cromwell' was also put out at 2130, but thankfully the scare passed and aircraft were stood down after this, one of many false invasion alerts throughout the war.

Gas

Standard Operating Practice for all AC squadrons included the laying of various types of gas, and in addition to the mustard stored in Mathams Wood other varieties arrived on the station. 22 September saw a large quantity of gas type S3D put into stock on the aerodrome, this being the harmless substance used by Army squadrons on exercise with the Army, and for the rest of the month 2 (AC) Squadron merrily sprayed infantry and armoured brigades of 2, 4 and 11 Corps with it daily during the course of training exercises at various locations throughout East Anglia. After 1942 the S3D gas was stored in a secure building, known for obscure reasons as the Smoke Curtain Installation (SCI) which was sited well off the eastern edge of the flying field to the north of a small wooded area near Henley Herne Spring. Access to it (Building 70) was via pass authority given at the SCI workshops (Building 69) to travel down the long concrete road which remained single-track with passing places throughout the war years.

Mathams Wood ALG Becomes RAF Sawbridgeworth

October 1940 was a very busy month for the staff section of 2 (AC) Squadron. 5 October saw an advance party from the squadron HQ, then still at Cambridge, arrive at Great Hyde Hall to establish the SHQ in readiness for the impending move of the whole squadron to the station. The hall (and cricket ground pavilion) had been earmarked for billets the previous month and with many bulldozers now levelling various areas of the estate grounds for hutting to be erected as accommodation and offices the gatehouse lodges became guard rooms. Security police started patrolling inside the estate perimeter railings, before these were taken away to be melted down for the war effort and replaced by barbed wire. The Ground Gunners were also tasked with perimeter defence here. At the end of a duty turn one of the Flight cleared his rifle in the guard room without realising that a round was in the chamber, and wounded the Guard Commander before the bullet also killed an off-duty soldier who was asleep in the room. Unfortunate incidents of this nature increased the serviceman's general awareness towards weapon handling.

Representatives from the Works Repair Depot, No 10 Area, at Harlow and the Ministry of Transport then visited the landing ground on 9 October with regard to the improvements necessary for a full-time occupation, and on the 14th the station Equipment Section was established at Townsend House and Glenroy, two large properties on London Road in the town centre taken over for the duration.

Coincident with all this activity the Luftwaffe then visited the area. A Heinkel He111 was shot down and crashed at Thorley Wash on 19 September, whilst on 10 October a lone raider dropped one very large bomb on the Cambridge Road which killed five people, and airmen plus the LDV toiled hard to help clear the debris. A Junkers Ju88 on another raid locally was hit by AA fire from Gaston Green site and crashed onto the Much Hadham Road on the 16th, whilst two parachute mines were dropped near Great Hyde Hall on the 18th. The first exploded and damaged windows at the Hall whilst the second fell into the river as a UXB, however when it was exploded by Royal Engineers the following day the blast blew 4 airmen at the Hall off their feet and caused more glass to be broken. Next day a stick of 9 bombs fell on the Great Hyde Hall cricket field itself and stopped play there for a while.

The crash of the Heinkel at Thorley Wash is remembered by Charles Mason who was at the time an instrument fitter with 2 (AC) Sqn and detailed for crash party duties that night. To reach the crash site, found to be a large crater near the river, the crew had to travel up the A11 then make their way across the railway line and full water meadows. The bodies of the three dead aircrew were removed and the crash party then stood guard throughout the night, which was one with a full moon and low cloudbase, and were kept alert by strong winds and ammunition exploding amongst the still-smouldering wreckage.

On 24 October 2 (AC) Squadron officially moved onto their new base, the Lysanders of all 3 flights arriving at intervals for dispersal around the south side of Newsett and Mathams Wood in a similar manner to the pre-war period. The operation went smoothly and was marred only by the communications aircraft, Moth Minor X5115 flown by Pilot Officer G Grant-Govan, disgracing itself by stalling in from 10' 0" and collapsing its undercarriage. Training at the new station was to have continued immediately after settling in but weather conditions in November were so bad that no flying was possible for half the month, indeed detachments sent to Caxton Gibbet in Cambridgeshire for night flying in order to escape the weather at home fared no better in trying to find more usable conditions.

As well as the usual exercises with local Army units on airfield defence and capture, which always happened soon after a new station was opened up, the first of the visitors appeared in the form of five pupil Army glider pilots. They arrived on 5 November for ab initio flying which was carried out in the Moth Minor by getting up to 2,000' and cutting the engine, then making an unpowered landing on the western grass area. When they left after a few days the Moth Minor was still in one piece.

At this time the station was still known to the Air Ministry as Mathams Wood, but upon 2 (AC) Squadron establishing itself there the Commanding Officer began referring to himself in correspondence as 'A J W Geddes, Wing Commander, OC No 2 (AC) Squadron – OC RAF Sawbridgeworth'. This caused concern in London and prompted numerous telephone calls to him demanding to know exactly what and where RAF Sawbridgeworth was. It took a lot of hard work by Geddes to convince the Air Ministry that the original LG was in the course of being enlarged to suit current requirements, but that they need not worry, the necessary work would be done using local labour quicker than the official channels could move in order that the squadron could get on with the war without having to wait.

A lot of the early buildings put up to serve the squadron were not passed for construction by the Air Ministry Works Department, but Geddes was not a pen pusher and believed in getting on with the job. Among the many local buildings acquired for use by the squadron was the Assembly Hall in Station Road which served as the cookhouse. This however was lost due to a fire there on 3 December and the facilities relocated in Church House the next day. The locations for a canteen and Army guardroom at Shingle Hall were agreed with the contractor on 13 December amidst initial objections by Mr Lukies, who was pacified when told that no military vehicles would be using the nearby main drive, but until the canteen opened Great Hyde Hall provided these facilities with the first Christmas dinner for airmen being held there on 25 December. Prior to wooden hutting arriving at Shingle Hall early in 1941 for mess rooms and other facilities, a mobile canteen was used on the site, such was Geddes' enthusiasm for giving his men what they needed.

Visitors

On 3 January 1941 Mr C J Incey of the Herts War Agricultural Committee visited the Station Offices with the misguided proposal that the aerodrome be ploughed up for crops. His ideas were not deemed conducive to flying operations therefore, after a fairly short meeting with the Officer Commanding, he was told quite firmly that he should go and plough up somewhere else.

The Luftwaffe marked the New Year by returning on 5 January when low-flying Ju88s once again attacked the area. Diving out of cloud the aircraft dropped many bombs on the western edge of the aerodrome close to the Flight Offices and dispersal areas but no casualties resulted and little damage was done except to crops on a number of farms.

Frost and heavy snow then meant no flying for a week but plenty of sweeping exercises, before dummy shoots were carried out on 13 January with the 53rd Heavy Artillery Regiment based near Bishops Stortford.

In between normal training the squadron always found time to entertain guests, one such being the Revd Davies of Sawbridgeworth. He lunched in the Officers' Mess on 16 January upon taking up his appointment as Station Chaplain, albeit only one squadron was there at that time. Church services were first held either at Great Hyde Hall, the Mission Hall at Green Tye or St Anne's Church, Allens Green until suitable facilities were made available on the airfield. On 12 October 1941 the first church services were held on the airfield in the NAAFI (Building 66), but when the combined chapel/gymnasium/cinema (Building 12) on the Communal Site was completed in May 1942 services were held there to include not only RAF personnel but others such as the National Fire Service from Sawbridgeworth town.

On 3 February 1941 an important visitor in the form of Colonel J L Kennedy, Air Liason Officer to the American Armed Forces, came for a 3-day tour of inspection. At a time when the USA was still neutral, but supportive of the British in spite of the "America for the Americans" lobby within their own country, his visit was seen as vital and necessary for good relations to exist between the two countries. Consequently he was treated to as grand a reception as the station could muster. Accompanied by (now) Squadron Leader Edinger he was met by a guard of honour at the SHQ at Great Hyde Hall where he started his tour. The following day he flew with W/C Geddes on a Lysander sortie over the Wash which demonstrated the extent of 2 (AC) Squadron's duties. Later that same day he was impressed by a set of oblique aerial photographs taken of the airfield, which had then been developed and printed in just 19 minutes during his presence.

Kennedy left the next day for London, which heralded the start of another period of no flying due to fog and snow. It was at this time that Air Ministry engineers surveyed an area on Blounts Farm to the south and east of the current landing ground in order that the airfield could be enlarged to Class A status. Whilst they did not know the anticipated use for the new site they quickly realised that the three runways planned for it did not match the existing layout put down under W/C Geddes' instructions. A further year was to elapse however before surveys and land aquisitions were complete in order to enlarge the aerodrome.

The first non-British aircraft arrived on 13 February when a Piper Cub brought in an Army major who was to participate in an 11 Corps exercise, and on 17 March four Naval Air Observers came for a one-week course on army co-operation.

Another visitor, this time a most distinguished one, came to view the work of 2 (AC) Squadron on 25 July 1941. Accompanied by AVM Sir Arthur Barratt KCB, CMG, MC, no less a personage than

Marshal of the RAF the Viscount Trenchard GCB, GCVO, DSO, DCL, LLD, the 'father' of the RAF, inspected and addressed the squadron. Four months previously AVM H C T Dowding, once the 'boss' of Fighter Command during the Battle of Britain, had come to assess the establishment state of 2 (AC) Squadron and left completely satisfied and suitably impressed.

An important visitor, and local resident, was Sir Archibald Sinclair who in his capacity as Secretary of State for Air inspected 'A' Flight, the Maintenance Flight and the airmen's cookhouse when he landed on 3 January 1942 accompanied by Group Captain Sir Louis Greig.

One visitor to cause some concern was F/Lt C D Hemet, DAPM Security of 23 Area, No 4 Region who presented himself on 30 October 1942. He spent some time at the guard room explaining why both his identity card and official permit were out of date before he was finally allowed onto the station to carry out his assessment tour.

Bed and Breakfast

From the time that more or less full-time occupancy of the expanded landing ground began in October 1940 with the arrival of 2 (AC) Squadron, until its reconstruction into a Class A site commencing in 1942, messing and living conditions were somewhat appalling. It was always expected that Army Co-operation squadrons should live 'rough' out in the field on exercises and it was never originally intended to raise the standard of the landing ground to anything other than just that. Air and ground crews were therefore given the minimum comforts, if comfort was the right phrase to use, by way of tents and the odd wooden hut on the grass areas which rapidly became a quagmire in anything but the best weather.

The winter of 1940/41 was a harsh one, and is particularly remembered for the amount of snow that fell. In these conditions the Lewis gun pits were manned 24 hours a day, by two airmen at a time generally on shifts of two hours on, four hours off, with only the sand-bags for protection against the cold, as well as the real enemy. One luxury the airmen had was a 'parenting' system, by which local residents offered a bath with a meal afterwards. A list of addresses was produced for them to contact locals to arrange a convenient night to visit, this arrangement continuing with bath parades to North Weald until the Communal Site facilities were complete later in the war.

The photographic, Air Intelligence Liason and payment/accounts offices meanwhile were set up in relative luxury at the already-existing buildings at Blounts and Shingle Hall farms (Buildings 32 & 19) where washing and catering facilities were on hand. The AIL had first occupied tents in the corner of the field near to the Defence HQ (Building 63) but moved into Blounts as soon as it became free.

As staffing levels and operational requirements rose to that more akin to a permanent establishment (with a total eventually reaching 996 RAF and 134 WAAF personnel) it was necessary to look further afield for billets, therefore numerous farms and private houses in the nearby town were requisitioned to fill the role. Although pilots were billeted in and around Station Road and Knight Street, and used farms at Bursteads and Three Mile Pond on the A11 in addition to hutting in the grounds of Great Hyde Hall, these were only temporary measures.

When the Officers' quarters and mess block on the east side of Parsonage Lane, opposite the Communal Site, were finished in 1942 these then provided the required space. Great Hyde Hall was first used as the SHQ, and throughout the war for accommodation, but whilst hutting was provided in the grounds for aerodrome staff and defence units the house itself was generally reserved for higher ranks and receiving visiting dignitaries. Geddes could easily have availed himself of these facilities but preferred to take a billet in Green Tye just to the west of the airfield.

When the dispersed accommodation sites received their full quota of airmen's billets in the form of standard Air Ministry timber hutting conditions improved, although it was found necessary in winter to send out foraging parties to local coalyards in order to supplement the meagre fuel allowances for

The cottages at Blounts Farm which served as the airfield defence force HQ in World War Two but are now occupied by farm employees.

When the Much Hadham Road was opened again to traffic postwar the stanchion and foundation of the westerly road barrier were uprooted. Put on the verge next to the Type FW3/24 pillbox just west of the approach to runway '13' they are still there.

2 (AC) Sqn Lysander passenger – 1940 style. Les Marriott wears issue boots, 1930 pattern Sidcot flying suit over battledress with tie, lightweight unframed Mk 3 goggles, 'D' type mask (chamois covered) and helmet type 'B' on camera aligment duty in Mk 2 Lysander N1262. His forage cap is on the tailplane.

Total weight of kit, without the 'Mae West' and parachute, is in the order of 10 lbs.

Aircraft AUW – 6015 lbs

(Compare dress with last photo in book.)

Les Marriott photo

Though not depicting 2 (AC) Squadron in one of its better moments, this shot of Tomahawk AH940, XV–U, at Thorley on 16 September 1941 does show the standard Fighter Command camouflage scheme with sky fuselage band and undersides plus the blue 'A' flight spinner tip colours.

D O Cook photo

the pot-bellied stoves. Apart from the social aspect of clustering round it to keep warm its only other use was to dry out wet clothing before the next duty, it never doing much towards warming up the hut interior.

Training on site

Much and varied was the training undertaken for A.C duties by the squadrons on site and at nearby locations. Although the flying field occupied a large area between Warren, Blounts and Shingle Hall Farms training needs sometimes took in other sites not in the control of the military at that time.

Message-dropping with marker streamers, the original and proven means of communication between air and ground units, had been carried out at Albury Hall but was practised at Sawbridgeworth by Lysanders and Tomahawks 'bombing' a marker cross in the field immediately north of Blounts Farm (exactly where the present Much Hadham Road passes Blounts Farm entrance). In both cases the messages were lobbed out of the cockpit, in the former by sliding back the canopy and for the latter by opening the direct vision sliding panel on the port side of the canopy. Message pick-ups on the Lysander only were achieved by means of the under-fuselage hook and practised on the side of the runway parallel to this area using a line suspended between two poles. This exercise went further to include the snatching of heavier items up to 10 lbs such as petrol cans, but their retrieval into the aircraft was difficult and dangerous therefore it was not pursued.

For bombing training, utilising 7½lb (later 11½) white smoke weapons released from the Lysander's stub wing racks, a large black square was put down in a rough grazing field to the east of Mathams Wood. Successful hits on this were viewed from an observation tower just to the north, as well as by local children in the Blounts Farm haystacks until they were ordered off.

It had been hoped to have a station rifle range and for this the gravel pit at Dane Bridge, two miles to the west on the Much Hadham Road, was inspected. As this only gave a range distance of 200 yards instead of the preferred 400 it was used infrequently in the hope that a more suitable location could be found. None was found and so in 1942 the 3-point machine-gun range (Building 40) was built as a substitute behind single-engined hardstand no 74/5 on the west side of Mathams Wood and used continually after that. A cannon test butt (Building 39) also in brick with sand infill was sited next to it.

From experience gained in France and the Low Countries it was apparent that the single Vickers gas-operated rear gun, fitted as original equipment to the Lysander, was totally inadequate for defence against faster enemy fighters. This situation was remedied in 1941 when twin .303" Brownings were fitted, work being carried out by Lundy Airlines at Barnstaple on two aircraft at a time, starting in late February.

Full anti-gas exercises were carried out fairly regularly in the early part of the war, using tear gas capsules to simulate an attack, and as an added encumbrance the wearing of gas masks (respirators) during routine servicing and bombing-up operations was a frequent diversion from the norm. Results were generally fair until a marked increase in the proper behaviour under gas conditions by a newly-arrived intake was found to be due to them wearing eye shields underneath their masks. Strangely enough, after this incident late in October 1941, no more anti-gas training exercises were held on the station . . .

An occasion of a reciprocal nature occurred that same month, when the Sawbridgeworth fire brigade used the facilities at Great Hyde Hall for a physical training session.

One activity not pursued on site was dinghy drill, even though a fair-sized lake existed in Mathams Wood. For this at least 24 lucky trainees at a time were loaded into a three-tonner along with up to five dinghies, and taken to Bishops Stortford where the Municipal Baths in The Causeway (now the site of the Library) were used.

Photographic work was the prime task for AC squadrons and required specialised training if good results were to be gained, to this end many practice sorties were undertaken in addition to operational flights. A sortie on 12 March 1942 of an extremely local nature comprised a vertical mosaic taken of Sawbridgeworth town by Lysanders of 2 (AC) Squadron, one of the last occasions on which the type was used before re-equipment with the Mustang commenced. The mosaic was framed and presented to the Town Council who still display it at their offices in Sayesbury Manor, Bell Street. Due to the 'flexibility' offered by the gunner/observer in the Lysanders many of the sorties could be carried out singly but later with the advent of the Mustang having fixed cameras and higher speed the pilot alone had to concentrate on the photo run. Lysanders, if attacked, could fly low and slow in and around ground features whilst the gunner fired, Mustang sorties being flown in pairs with the leader taking the pictures covered by his number 2. The hand-held cameras used in the Lysanders gave way to fixed F24 in the faster types and were operated by a pushbutton on the control column. Mounted in the fuselage behind the pilot to fire out to port these took rear-facing oblique (RFO) shots using a 5in x 5in (127mm square) film of either 125 or 250 exposures, aiming being by means of an alignment mark painted on the trailing edge of the port wing. The Spitfires used a similar arrangement, with the camera mounted in the rear fuselage, but when the Mosquito PR16 came into use with its array of forward-facing, vertical and oblique cameras the navigator's job, with the pilot established on the photo run, was to keep a rearward look-out. In the event of the Mosquito being chased by fast German types the navigator would kneel facing aft on the wing spar and direct the pilot on the best evasive tactics to use prior to him avoiding interception by employing the high speed characteristics the type was renowned for.

Squadrons based on, or detached to, the station participated in many exercises with the army. Those involving the 'home base' included 'Lively' on 11 June 1942 plus 'Bury' and 'Limpet' between 1–17 July, whilst others included 'Blitz, Bullets, Bumper, Filter, Jungle, Scorch, Simple 2 and Walton'. Most of the AC squadrons in the UK took part in the largest of all, 'Spartan', which in March 1943 involved all three services and required the aircraft to operate out of temporary tracked airstrips laid down in Berkshire by the newly-formed Airfield Construction Groups. This was a rehearsal for 'Overlord', the invasion of Europe, one operation in which no aircraft from Sawbridgeworth took part for by that time the station was devoid of resident squadrons.

Recreation

In late 1940, during the early days of the first 'permanent' squadron, off-duty time was generally spent in the time-honoured tradition of card schools, writing letters home or frequenting the local pubs, due to the initial lack of social facilities on the airfield itself.

At this time Sawbridgeworth had some 13 inns, whilst Green Tye, Spellbrook and High Wych had two each, and Allens Green (the closest) had one. Great Hyde Hall staff had the Railway Inn practically at the bottom of the front drive, this no doubt was used heavily on 20 October 1940 when German bombs ruined the cricket field and spoilt chances of any relaxation there.

The pilots tended to go further afield for refreshment, such as Bishops Stortford or across the county boundary to Harlow Mill or Potter Street, whilst the ground crews finished off their evening's work with a brisk walk either to the Queen's Head at Allens Green, the Bull on Cambridge Road or the White Horse in Green Tye (now a private house).

Travelling shows such as the Entertainments National Service Association (ENSA, or 'Every Night Something Awful') visited, the first being in Harlow on 10 December 1940 and the second in the SHQ itself on 21 January 1941 when all ranks attended. Three days later by way of a variation the SHQ hosted a concert by the band of the Royal Corps of Signals.

Along with the facilities offered at the United Services Club in Station Road the cinema was another form of entertainment. Sawbridgeworth had its own in Sayesbury Road (now the Roman Catholic church) whilst Bishops Stortford had three to choose from, until the multi-purpose Building 12 (gymnasium/chapel/theatre) on the Communal Site was built in 1942. The Congregational church in South Street became the original Bishops Stortford cinema, but this closed in 1932 and re-opened as the Phoenix in 1935. Nearby the Regent and Empire also opened in 1935 on opposite sides of the road, but whilst the former became the Granada the others turned their attentions in the 1960s to the bingo trade.

Boat trips on the River Stort were also popular, as was swimming until one man, LAC J Dodds, drowned and all ranks were then restricted to using the Municipal Baths in Bishops Stortford. The lake in Mathams Wood was technically an additional fire pool but it also provided some entertainment when iced over in winter and could be 'skated' on if the thickness was enough to take weight but, as AC2 Sid Napier found to his cost when he fell through in the course of a bet to cross it, English ice is not as thick as it seems.

Until the wood became full up with gas bombs and other munitions a favourite pastime was rabbit shooting, both for sport and as a way of increasing the meagre wartime rations. When W/C Geddes went to London on 15 March 1941 to receive his OBE from the King for 'special services to aviation' the pilots of 2 (AC) Squadron decided to have a shoot that day in celebration of the event. These were popular with all, except 'C' flight commander George Kenning who had the misfortune to shoot himself in the foot on one occasion.

November 1941 saw the Sergeants' mess for 2 (AC) Squadron hold a successful dance at Long's Cafe, Bishops Stortford in order to raise money for the Squadron's compassionate fund, whilst the Officers Mess used the more salubrious facilities offered by Great Hyde Hall for their Christmas dinner. In December it was mooted that a large barn to the north-west of Shingle Hall be used as the station theatre, but no record of events put on there has survived. This was one of the two barns taken over by the Air Ministry prior to the management of Walter Lawrences factory in the town offering the use of their recreation room, the United Services Club in Station Road becoming available and the single squash court (Building 22) being completed on the Communal Site.

Highway Men

Although the station was on the Air Ministry books as regards the supply of material for military purposes, it was left to the QM staff to arrange for everyday items to be brought in. Prior to the mains being laid onto the airfield in March 1942 it was standard practice to send a lorry towing a bowser into the town to collect water for general uses. On one such trip to the well in West Road on 21 September 1941 the combination failed to clear the road bend at Allens Green church and ran over a 15 year old local child. The girl, Doris Bird, died and was buried in Bishops Stortford, the funeral being attended by a number of the station personnel.

Another incident resulting in a fatality occurred on 22 November 1941 when the Station Despatch Rider, AC1 L E K Lax, ran into a parked lorry whilst returning from a duty run to North Weald. The use of DRs for mail collection and other tasks was commonplace but this was the only one from the station to come to grief.

Throughout the war supplies of coal were obtained from North Weald by road. The lorries used were military Crossley 3-tonners with the addition of a gunner's hatch in the cab roof and a Lewis gun mounted there. Ken Bell remembers that, as a Ground Gunner, it was his job throughout the journey to travel standing on the passenger seat with his head stuck out of the hatch to man the gun. No instances are recorded however of the gunner having to use his weapon to protect the cargo against attack from 'bandits' lying in wait, although on one occasion one lorry-load had to be transferred to another after it was in accidental collision with a local haulier's lorry in Mill Hill, Sawbridgeworth.

Naturally, as it was heavily rationed, many people were involved in the misuse of military petrol. A prime example was the batman to one of the Air Intelligence Officers, who somehow managed to get enough of the standard 4-gallon packs to the Acme Garage in Bishops Stortford where he sold it for 30/– (£1.50) per pack. Another friendly airman got local man Len Eve free petrol for his car, but it wouldn't run properly after that on the military 'red stuff'.

On another occasion, whilst on the way home one evening, W/C Geddes' car, a little 2-seater given to him by the RAF servicemen at Bekesborne for his work in France, ran out of petrol on the aerodrome. Whilst pondering what to do some airmen appeared and offered him some petrol on the proviso that Geddes give them a lift into the town. After filling him up they were given a lift to the local police station and reported for misuse of military fuel!

Aircraft cleaning was one activity where the improper use of petrol was allowed. A mix of 100 Octane and 'Persil' removed dirt from the Lysander underside very nicely, then a wipe over with an oily rag helped polish it up to a shiny finish. AC2 Sid Napier (fitter, A2 grade on Lysanders) recalls that neat 100 Octane also cleaned out oil and grease from uniform tunics if they were hung from trees in Mathams Wood whilst the wearer stood in his underwear pouring petrol on and brushing it through until the stains disappeared. Needless to say, smoking was banned during and after this exercise!

Natural changes

Within Mathams Wood a demi-paradise of nature had existed prior to the military taking over the airfield. Many locals had carried out nature studies on the flora and fauna here, and children knew it as a grassy place always full of bluebells in the summer, but all this changed with the arrival of the military who fenced it off to the public and turned it into a veritable arsenal with hazardous substances stored in it. In the wood was a fair-sized lake that had been fished by Rover Scouts from Bishops Stortford who camped at Newsett in the early 1930s, this lake being doubled in size in 1943 to act as an emergency water supply for that part of the airfield. The wooded area was somewhat higher than the surrounding fields but the lake was, and still is, full even in the driest seasons. Natural drainage down to Fiddlers Brook was the norm, supplemented by mole drainage in the area between Mathams Wood and the Much Hadham Road put in by steam ploughs in 1926. This took ground water to a ditch which originally ran along the north side of the road then turned south towards Sweetdews Lane, but this ditch disappeared when the trackways running NW–SE and N–S were laid down in 1941, as did part of the south-west corner of the wood. A wind-pump near Sacombs Ash used to pump water from Fiddlers Brook up to Blounts Farm, but this too was removed as being a hazard to flying when the longer NW–SE run was in use from 1942 onwards.

When the building contractors, W C French & Co and the Air Ministry Works Department, carried out works on perimeter track, aircraft pens and various buildings in and around the wood in 1942 natural watercourses and ditches were diverted or blocked. The corner of the wood surrounding the site of 'Mathams' was cut back due to it falling within a runway clearance area, and the part-filling of the moat caused extensive water-logging to occur in the better seasons of the year as well as during the normally wet winter months. When Sommerfeld track runways were laid in 1942 other parking areas were also given the benefit of metal tracking which helped reduce the quagmire effect.

From 1940 until 1943 the southern fringe of the wood was home to the bomb and petrol stores which were in open compounds again under the tree canopy, where no aircraft dispersals were sited. The petrol store consisted of pile upon pile of 4-gallon packs (2x2 gallon cans in cardboard cases) but when the airfield was enlarged in 1942 fuel storage was upgraded by two fixed 24,000 gallon capacity installations (Buildings 28 & 29) at separate locations west of Blounts Farm and north of Shingle Hall. The location of the former is recognisable today as a large earth mound covering the tank surrounded by a wire fence, whilst the latter is only visible by the remains of its access road forming a layby on the Much Hadham Road. A third installation (Building 30) of 5000 gallons capacity for motor transport was sited near the main stores on the Shingle Hall technical site.

Road changes in the Second World War

The Much Hadham to Trims Green road had traffic controls placed on it from 1940 until 1942, when aircraft were using the two steel mat runways which ran both parallel and up to it near Shingle Hall, by wooden barriers at Trims Green (manned amongst others by ex-steam plough driver Julius Holder, now in the LDV) and Fiddlers Brook. From 1942 these became 'permanent' barriers when the runway clearance areas were laid out, farmers and locals having business on the land then required passes to travel along the road.

The Assembly Hall, Sawbridgeworth. Removed from the Communal Site in 1947 then re-erected in The Forbury it was, in its former life, the chapel/gymnasium/theatre but has since been extended and forms a lasting memorial to all those from the town who lost their lives in two world wars. Near the memorial plaques in the foyer is a piece of stone from the 1941 bombing of the Houses of Parliament. (Yes, it was snowing!)

The United Services Club in Station Road (previously the Shaftesbury Hall) provided relaxation for servicemen in two world wars and continues in the same role today for civilians.

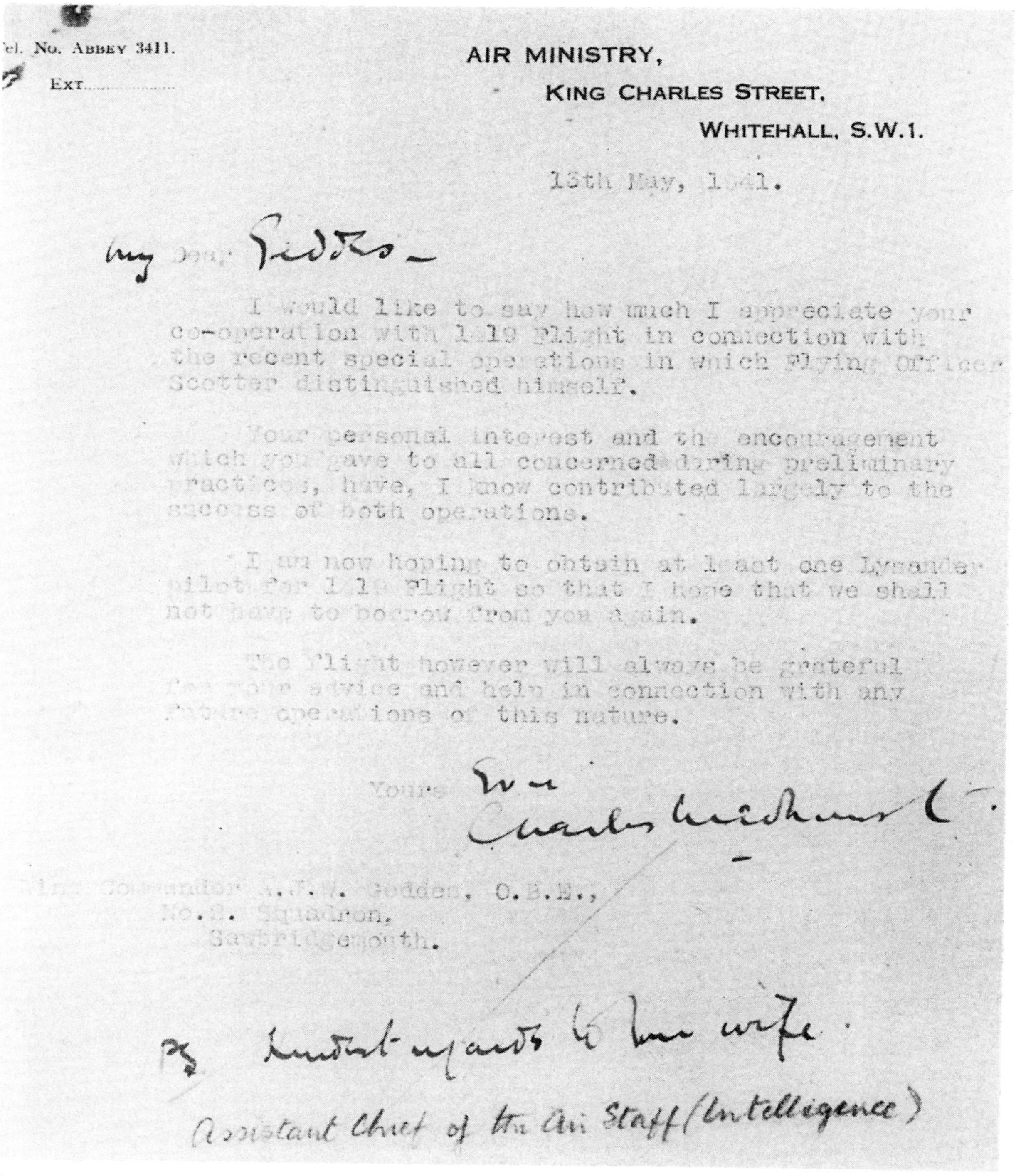

Tel. No. Abbey 3411.

Ext............

AIR MINISTRY,

KING CHARLES STREET,

WHITEHALL, S.W.1.

13th May, 1941.

My dear Geddes —

    I would like to say how much I appreciate your co-operation with 1419 Flight in connection with the recent special operations in which Flying Officer Scotter distinguished himself.

    Your personal interest and the encouragement which you gave to all concerned during preliminary practices, have, I know contributed largely to the success of both operations.

    I am now hoping to obtain at least one Lysander pilot for 1419 Flight so that I hope that we shall not have to borrow from you again.

    The Flight however will always be grateful for your advice and help in connection with any future operations of this nature.

Yours ever

Charles Medhurst

Wing Commander A.J.W. Geddes, O.B.E.,
No.2 Squadron,
Sawbridgeworth.

PS kindest regards to your wife.

(Assistant Chief of the Air Staff (Intelligence))

The letter of thanks from the Air Ministry, sent to Andrew Geddes after the second long-distance flight carried out by Gordon Scotter for SOE, acknowledging the help given by 2 (AC) Squadron. Although a formal communication note the personal sentiments included in what is an historic document.

As noted on the original letter, Charles Medhurst was at the time Assistant Chief of the Air Staff (Intelligence), but had been OC of 4 Squadron (another of the Army's Co-operation units) from 1930–31.

Photo via 2 (AC) Squadron library

The road running north to Blounts Cottages from its junction with Sacombs Ash Lane (a tollgate having previously been there) was at this time still a private trackway and as such no restrictions could be put on its use. As no great amount of traffic except that using Blounts Farm was expected to reach the Much Hadham Road by this route it was taken over in 1942 when the full airfield layout was realised and not re-opened to the public until March 1946, by which time it had become officially adopted.

When the full airfield layout with three Sommerfeld mesh runways and concrete perimeter track was disclosed it was apparent that the clearance area for the longest runway, that running parallel to the Much Hadham Road, extended over the road line at the approach to '13'. Accordingly the road bends here were straightened out by a new section built in mid-March 1943 from halfway between Fiddlers Brook and the entrance to Blounts Farm. At the west end of this section the road barrier was relocated and a guard pillbox erected.

A further road was laid across the fields to the south to link up with Sacombs Ash Lane where it had previously finished at Sacombs Ash House. This was required, along with Sweetdews Lane and the Trims Green to Rook End section, to act as a bypass for the airfield but was taken up post-war when the fields returned to farmland. With the final enlargements and improvements to the airfield in 1942 Blounts Farm ended up encircled by perimeter track within the airfield, and remained so for the rest of the war.

The rising of the Moon Squadrons

It is not widely known that 2 (AC) Sqn, while based at Sawbridgeworth, played the major part in initial training of SOE Lysander pilots who were to be operating the type on pick-up duties in and out of Occupied France.

The use of the Lysander as an ideal vehicle for clandestine trips to the Continent was first demonstrated, unofficially, on 3 September 1940 when W/C Geddes went from Newmarket to Tours in Western France to deliver an agent to a reception committee there. So secret was this mission that no mention was made in the Squadron Operations Record Books, and even Geddes' own log book merely calls it a 'long range air test'.

On 19/20 October 1940 the second (but officially the first) pick-up was made by F/Lt W R Farley in Lysander R9029 when he collected Philip Schneidau, an SIS agent. The pick-up, made south of Fontainebleau, Montigny was successful but Farley became lost during bad weather on the return flight and eventually landed out of fuel at Connel, Oban where the aircraft was destroyed when it hit anti-invasion defences.

Nevertheless by the success of this mission the pick-up concept was established and, in December 1940, Geddes was requested by the Air Ministry to select a small number of very good pilots, give them no details of what they might be required to do but have them practise short field landings and take-offs at night under his supervision.

Geddes picked P/Os Scotter and Robinson, plus F/Lts Chapman and Houseman then, on 30 December an officer from HQ 71 Group presented himself at SHQ as S/L E V Knowles. 'Teddy' Knowles was at that time C/O of 419 Flight at North Weald, itself a spurious title for a unit that would eventually change to 1419 Flight and become 138 (Special Duties) Squadron, and gave Geddes details of the special job in which the help of 2 (AC) Squadron would be vital. He wanted the chosen pilots to be able to land a Lysander on the smallest piece of ground in any weather situation but especially on moonless nights or in overcast conditions. They were to be able to navigate without errors, land and take off unaided, but not know for the present what the 'job' entailed.

Training began on 8 January 1941, using the area of the 1937 landing ground with slow approaches being made over Newsett and Mathams Wood onto the landing area which was marked only by the light of 3 cycle lamps bought in the town and positioned in the shape of a 'L' pointing down-wind as a 150 yard long flarepath. Initially the SOE trainees used standard 2 (AC) Squadron Lysanders painted black over-all but, after it was found that the silhouette was easily seen under certain moon conditions, the upper surfaces were repainted in the normal camouflage for the period.

At the end of February 1941 Knowles came again to discuss further the use of Lysander pilots from 2 (AC) Squadron in SOE work and, upon his departure, work continued with the pilots now knowing what the new job entailed. Flying intensified until the pilots became proficient in it, however F/O A E Houseman broke the run of good luck when he dropped Lysander T1696 in heavily one evening but neither pilot or machine suffered much damage. The results of Geddes' training were then realised on 11 April when Gordon Scotter took V9287 (a Mk 2) on a long range flight to north of Chateauroux, between Levroux and Brion, in Occupied France to collect a 'Lt Cartwright'. Staging was via Tangmere with Scotter's aircraft mounting a long-range fuel tank, plus blackout curtains and basic ladder access to the rear cockpit.

In addition to the pilots under training for (now) 1419 Flight at Sawbridgeworth one was collected from Martlesham Heath on 21 May by Geddes in a 2 (AC) Squadron Tiger Moth. The new man, F/O J Nesbitt-Dufort, received a 1419 Flight Lysander, R2626, and for the rest of the month practised until he was able to get airborne in under 36 yards even in the muddy conditions persisting at Sawbridgeworth. R2626 was the only Lysander with 1419 Flight at that time (it eventually had six) but was not used on the next flight into France, nor was it a specially modified one.

The appearance of 'black' Lysanders was something of a mystery to other RAF personnel who were not 'in the know' but came into contact with them in the course of their normal duties. One such person was Cpl Alan Webb who, whilst in charge of the Station Flight at Hornchurch on 10 May 1941, was told to fill up the tanks of a Lysander that landed there and not ask any questions of the occupants. He couldn't help noticing, however, the black overalls worn by the pilot and the rear access ladder but assumed that it was an Army Co-operation aircraft as it had stub wings fitted. He guessed rightly from the amount of petrol required that it had already carried out its duties and needed to return to its own base, but no indications were given as to where it had been, what it was doing or where it was going back to. When refuelling was completed Scotter emerged from the watch office and took off for return to Sawbridgeworth at the end of this, his second flight for SOE/DDI. His passenger this time was 'F/Lt Phillipson', the RAF cover name for Philip Schneidau, who had been picked up from the edge of a forest at Fontainebleau near to where he had been staying whilst operating in the area.

On 21 May Scotter was awarded an immediate DFC for his work in this important new field. The award was received at a special function held at Great Hyde Hall where he, along with Chapman and Houseman, was presented to Field Marshal Sir Alan Brooke, Chief of the Imperial General Staff, who visited Sawbridgeworth to view at close hand the SOE pilot training being carried out there.

Whilst many stories abounded as to what all this training was for, the pilots gave nothing away. What was noticed by other squadron members were the nameless faces posted in who had no hand in daily duties, or no 'ground job', and many were the insults that were hurled at them for being apparently part-time fliers. One in particular, Roman Czerniawski (code name 'Armand'), caused Geddes concern when he entered the Hyde Hall mess and from out of his coat produced a copy of the previous day's *Paris Soir* newspaper which he had brought back on his latest pick-up. It was quickly hidden by Geddes, but this kind of error under relaxed conditions was fortunately rare.

After these episodes the SD Lysander Mk 3 was prepared under Air Ministry contract SCW (Special Contract-Westland) by Fairfield Aviation at White Waltham who carried out the necessary modifications. In addition to the standard 98-gallon inboard fuel tank an under-fuselage overload tank of 150 gallons capacity was fitted between the undercarriage legs which increased the flight duration to 10 hours and the range to 1150 miles.

An external access ladder fixed on the port fuselage side for rapid exit/entry to the rear cockpit had the ladder rungs picked out in yellow for easier location in the dark, and the stub wings were removed. A fixed locker was installed under the agent's rearward-facing seat for stowing packages but, apart from a radio link with the pilot, generally no other equipment usually configured was fitted. All these changes were found by experience to be useful aids to the job.

Upon completion of the SOE flying training programme John Nesbitt-Dufort returned to 1419 Flight, taking with him three of the trainees but leaving Gordon Scotter to stay at Sawbridgeworth with 2 (AC) Squadron. Houseman returned to the squadron later, having carried out no operations with SOE. In August 1941 1419 Flight was based at Newmarket and still commanded by Knowles, who had by now ascended to Wing Commander rank, it then renumbered as 138 (Special Duties) Squadron and thus ended its connections with Sawbridgeworth.

Troublesome times with the Tomahawk

An inkling of what was to happen with regard to re-equipment for Army Co-operation squadrons occurred on 23 May 1941, when one of the 2 (AC) Squadron Lysander wireless sets was sent to Henlow to be fitted into a Curtiss Tomahawk. This was one of a batch received in England from USAAF stocks which had been tested at the Air Fighting Development Unit and found lacking on a pure fighter basis, when compared to current enemy aircraft on equal terms, therefore storage was deemed the answer until they were eventually used for training or overseas work.

Further confirmation that Tomahawks were to be received at Sawbridgeworth came on 7 June when surveyors from Army Co-Operation Command and No 10 Works Area at Harlow inspected the airfield. This was the first step prior to the necessary replacement of the coir matting with something more substantial for Tomahawks, and on 16 June the first of some 200 men from the Aerodrome Maintenance Company arrived to be put under canvas accommodation.

Airfield reconstruction work duly started with two 150' 0" wide Sommerfeld track strips being laid, initially one at a length of 1300 yards on headings of 13/31 to replace the single coir mat run followed by a second at 1000 yards on headings of 02/20. The clearance area for the latter run crossed the Much Hadham Road at its southern end and necessitated traffic controls when flying was in progress. A 40' 0" wide perimeter track was laid out in mesh to serve the new 02/20 run with the Much Hadham Road serving as a taxiway between its end near Shingle Hall and the dispersals near Blounts Farm. A single Blister hangar for workshops was sited to the north-east of the runway intersection (close to where Blister 82/5 was placed when the 1942 enlargements were completed) and was the only permanent structure built at this time. The total area of land now under Air Ministry control on the airfield site, including the 62 acres of both Newsett and Mathams Wood, had increased to 280 acres.

In the meantime on 26 June the CO and two officer pilots from 2 (AC) Squadron went to Old Sarum for a conversion course on the Tomahawk. Three more pilots went on the 29th, and 2 July also, but conversion was slow, however on 18 August Tomahawk instructors came to Sawbridgeworth in Harvards to clear all those who had been on the course.

With the 'buzz' going round that high-speed aircraft were to be based at Sawbridgeworth, the Commanding Officer of RAF North Weald called on 15 August to ascertain whether the aerodrome could be used as a satellite for pure fighter operations. He was told, however, that Army Co-operation duties had first call on the facilities and went away disgruntled.

On 22 August the first two Tomahawks for 2 (AC) Sqn were collected from Cunliffe Owen Aircraft at Old Sarum, with a further two brought in on the 24th. With the arrival of the fifth aircraft on 27 August the instructors returned to clear a further three pilots to fly the type, a total of 12 from the squadron now being so authorised.

In the meantime, on 25 August, 241 and 268 Squadrons arrived to join No 2 (AC) for exercises with 11 Corps. All three units were still operating the Lysander as well as the Tomahawk and by the end of the exercises continual use had been made of the Sommerfeld tracking, an officer from the USAAF duly inspecting the surface for rate of wear. The results were deemed satisfactory, although this assessment was made under conditions of good weather and not the inclement type that brought

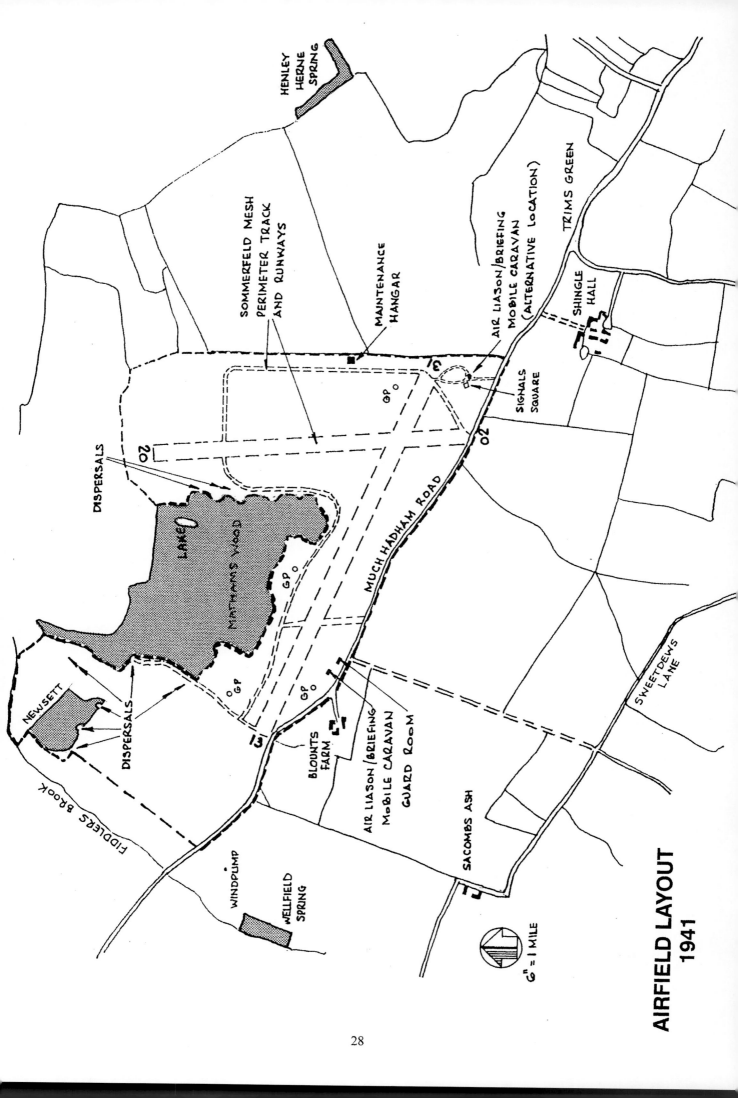

HENLEY HERNE SPRING

SOMMERFELD MESH PERIMETER TRACK AND RUNWAYS

MAINTENANCE HANGAR

AIR LIASON/BRIEFING MOBILE CARAVAN (ALTERNATIVE LOCATION)

TRIMS GREEN

SHINGLE HALL

SIGNALS SQUARE

GP

DISPERSALS

LANE

NATHAN'S WOOD

MUCH HADHAM ROAD

GP

GP

NEWSETT

DISPERSALS

GP

GP

BLOUNTS FARM

AIR LIASON/BRIEFING MOBILE CARAVAN

GUARD ROOM

SACOMBS ASH

SWEETDEWS LANE

FIDDLERS BROOK

WINDPUMP

WELLFIELD SPRING

6" = 1 MILE

AIRFIELD LAYOUT
1941

about frequent spells of airfield unserviceability due to the light runway construction on a clayey strata.

There then followed a spate of accidents with Tomahawks of 2 (AC) Squadron. Ground-loops occurred on the runway tracking on 9, 10 and 12 September, with engine failures on 16 and 18 September. This brought the decision that all were to be grounded until the generator gear drives (which had caused the engine failures) were rectified, and the pilots' general attitude to what they considered an inferior American product also changed.

Whilst the type offered great improvements over the Lysander, in terms of speed, fixed cameras and offensive armament, the many and varied negative comments received were not conducive to good relations between the British and Americans, therefore the Tomahawk was withdrawn from A.C use at Sawbridgeworth and the trusty Lysander put back into service until all problems with the Tomahawk were resolved. This was not to happen and, whilst some were sent back to Cunliffe Owen in October for flame damper modifications and duly returned to carry out the occasional solo night flight, use of the type in the European theatre was finally phased out by April 1942 without ever going into action. The Lysander therefore soldiered on until the arrival in late April 1942 of another, better, product of the American aircraft industry which suited the task ideally – the North American Mustang.

2 (AC) Squadron carried on with its exercises using the Lysander, in parallel with the Tomahawk, on the next phase of A/C training. This was Exercise 'Bumper', which ran from 29 September until 3 October, and involved the squadron operating from another airfield and treating its own as if it had been recently captured. Detached to Wattisham in Suffolk the squadron repeatedly occupied its 'home' base, leaving only when the 'enemy' troops defending it were deemed to have over-run it.

Lights, camera, action!

As most PR and Tac/R sorties from Sawbridgeworth were commenced with a take-off time often early in the morning, or with returns at dusk, it was apparent that some form of airfield lighting was required. On 18 October 1941 the Electrical Engineering Officer for No 10 Works Area, Mr Pallott, inspected the site and proposed the installation of a Drem Mk 2 system for runway and taxi-ways. Power was to be drawn direct from the National Grid by a switch system and thence to the airfield on overhead poles before being routed underground to the runways, control for the pattern required being managed by the watch office, but when the standby set house was built in 1942 it then took over from the grid.

No records giving the extent of the system installed have been found but examination of the full airfield layout on aerial photographs shows flarepaths to all three runways, as well as limited fog funnel lights, and taxi lights to the perimeter track. The system was only activated on a few occasions, as noted by the late Doris Barker of Thorley Lane who lived close to where Gordon Scotter's Tomahawk force-landed on 16 September 1941.

Runway flarepath lights were the cast iron type C6 with double white 40W pygmy lamps placed singly on concrete bases set flush with the tracking at 100 yd intervals, the end 400 yds being in blue, both sides of the runway. Across the runway in use, 800 yds from the upwind end, was a 'crossbar' of type C5 blue 40W lamps with five on the runway and one each side on the grass as a cautionary zone. The perimeter track lights were the multiple-aperture single type T1 with 15W lamps spaced at 150 yards, showing blue onto the taxiway and amber onto the grass, with closer spacing on bends and a pair at the holding point just before entering the runway itself.

Much evidence still exists of the Drem Mk 2 system by way of C5 and C6 lamps uprooted and, along with their concrete bases, dumped in Mathams Wood. Similarly the twin sockets in concrete bases at each runway end for powering the mobile floodlight and obstruction light have also been unearthed. Nothing however has been found to support the existence of outer circle lighting placed in adjacent fields to act as lead-ins to the lighted runway or 'totem poles', the two sets of six vertical

AIRCRAFT PEN – BLENHEIM TYPE 7181/41
(building 61/9)

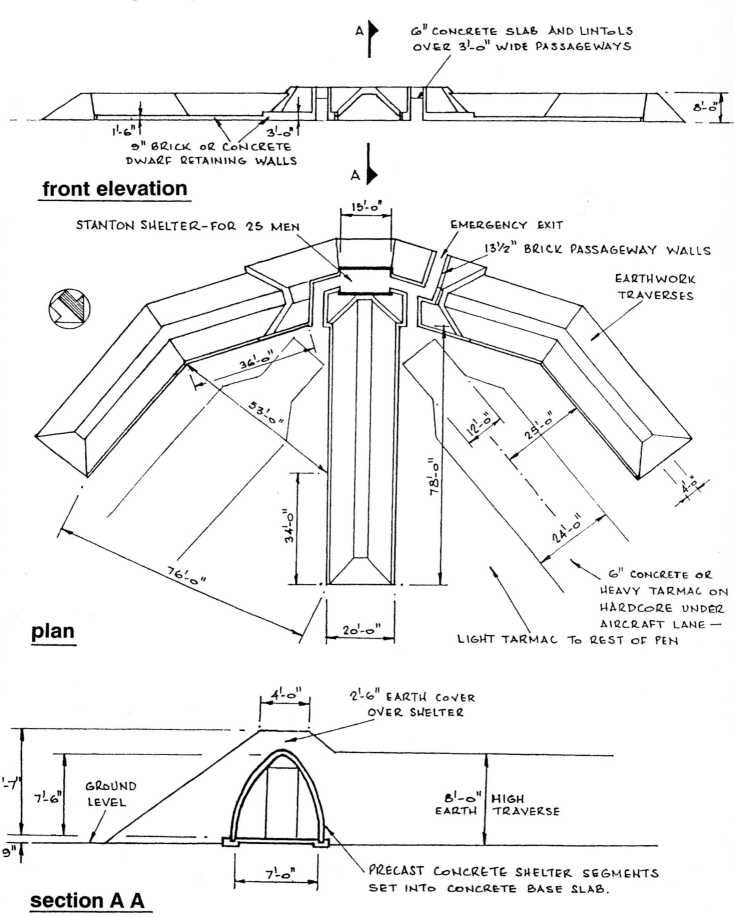

A ▶ 6" CONCRETE SLAB AND LINTOLS OVER 3'-0" WIDE PASSAGEWAYS

8'-0"

1'-6"   3'-0"

9" BRICK OR CONCRETE DWARF RETAINING WALLS

A ▶

front elevation

15'-0"

STANTON SHELTER – FOR 25 MEN

EMERGENCY EXIT

13½" BRICK PASSAGEWAY WALLS

EARTHWORK TRAVERSES

36'-0"

53'-0"

12'-0"

25'-0"

78'-0"

34'-0"

4'-0"

24'-0"

76'-0"

20'-0"

6" CONCRETE OR HEAVY TARMAC ON HARDCORE UNDER AIRCRAFT LANE —

LIGHT TARMAC TO REST OF PEN

plan

4'-0"

2'-6" EARTH COVER OVER SHELTER

GROUND LEVEL

1'-7"

7'-6"

8'-0" HIGH EARTH TRAVERSE

9"

7'-0"

PRECAST CONCRETE SHELTER SEGMENTS SET INTO CONCRETE BASE SLAB.

section A A

Scale 1:330

lights on poles 450 feet apart to mark the extent of the safe overrun for each runway end. As these lights were normally on wooden poles outside the airfield boundary, and timber was in short supply postwar, it is possible that they have 'walked'.

RAF Sawbridgeworth – the final phase

Whilst the addition of Sommerfeld mesh to two runways and the perimeter track in June of 1941 had been a great improvement over the previous grass surface landing and taxi-ing in inclement weather was still a problem. In order therefore to eliminate the tendancy for ground-looping Tomahawks to tear out a section of mesh and create a ball of knitting the runways were restructured at the end of September. After lifting sections of mesh the ground was scraped and a layer of large stone compacted in. Two further layers of progressively smaller stones were then added, before coir matting was relaid and mesh stretched over the top. Once all these materials were in place the top was finished off using a quick-drying cement grout to fill the voids in the matting, and thus achieve a very durable and reliable runway. The mesh perimeter track was given a similar treatment which started on 10 October.

Tomahawks were not the only machines to have had problems on the runway tracking. At the end of December 1941 trials with the airfield snow plough, a Bunce type mounted on a 3-ton Bedford truck, elicited the results that it worked well on test sections of Army Track but not on Sommerfeld. Nevertheless the latter type of track continued to be used and after placing extra picketing the Bunce machine performed adequately.

When the brick and concrete aircraft hardstands and pens were started on the east side of the airfield on 30 December 1941 it was decided to provide a concrete perimeter track as well in order to obviate the old problems of mud and water-logging restricting aircraft movements. It was also agreed that the three-runway layout be started as soon as possible, although this would again be laid in Sommerfeld Tracking, and 2 (AC) Squadron (the only unit on the station at that time) would stay in residence throughout the re-building phase

RAF Regiment

Airfield defences also changed at this time. Previously Ground Gunners seconded from the RAF had manned guns for anti-aircraft tasks since 1940, some 35,000 being spread around 365 UK airfields as detached flights by the start of that year, but on 1 February 1942 the RAF Regiment was formed with a strength of some 66,000 men to take over completely the responsibility for all aspects of airfield defence. The original Defence Squadrons that took over from Army units were numbered 701 to 850 in December 1941, but renumbered 2701 to 2850 as the first RAF Regiment squadrons whilst the independent flights were numbered from 4001 to 4336. As the need arose they were supplemented by the Army, either for the supply of manpower or AA weapons.

2770 Sqn RAFR reformed at Sawbridgeworth on 1 February 1942 from 770 Defence Squadron as a light AA unit, with one officer and 60 airmen manning its twelve 20mm Hispano guns. It had previously established airfield AA and perimeter works so, under its new title, concentrated on field defences, ground-to-air firing at West Mersea and Clacton, and musketry(!) courses on the ranges at Youngsbury near High Cross on the A10. After seeing in a new airfield layout, Mustangs and the first stay by Fleet Air Arm detachments it left on 30 September for the RAF Regiment depot at Grantham, eventually transferring to 2nd TAF in April 1944.

Rebuilding

The contract for enlarging the airfield and providing permanent facilities on new technical and dispersed sites was awarded to W C French & Co on 9 March 1942, the first workers from the company offices at Buckhurst Hill, Essex, arriving on 14 March. Work started first in the area of the

Communal Site when the approach road to the WAAF site was set out across common field no 16, previously known as 'Underlands'.

Work in the area of the Communal Site itself commenced on 15 March, with the new and novel feature of piped water appearing in the form of a 4" (100mm) diameter main being laid to the site from the A11 (Sawbridgeworth-Bishops Stortford) road on 20 March.

Finding, and hiding, the airfield

As an aid to locating the airfield when aircraft were lost, or under bad weather conditions, a VHF/DF (Very High Frequency/Direction-Finding) system was installed to the west of the approach to runway '13'. Work by Marconi in fitting the set-up commenced on 28 January 1942, and it was intended to be a boon to bad weather operations but subsequent events proved this not to be so. The DF apparatus was housed in a wooden ten-sided 'igloo' structure with small windows which was intended to be blast-proof although it was never put to the test. The operators were billeted in a nearby brick hut, which remains in place today by the roadside leading to Warren Farm, having been home in recent years to local tramps and vagrants but is now boarded up. In the middle of the field formed by the nearby crossroads a searchlight position was located, in conjunction with the DF site.

When the equipment was removed post-war Geoff Ashwell, at nearby Warren Farm, laid first claim to the wooden building as timber was in short supply and asked the RAF not to demolish it but let him take it away. Some portions of the hut are still doing service at Warren Farm even now.

31 January 1942 saw a visit from P/O Hawksley of Colonel Turner's Camouflage Section, and the suggestion that the growing aerodrome be afforded the protection of a decoy site. As similar topography had been found six miles due east at Great Canfield it was proposed, and agreed by the Station Comander, S/L K K Horn, that a Drem 'Q' site be put there. Notwithstanding this agreement no records exist to confirm that it was in fact ever used, although one suspiciously military-looking building exists at MR TL 571196 by the side of the road leading north into Puttocks End from Great Canfield. What Great Canfield residents do recall is that in 1943, en route to an emergency landing at Stansted, a Lancaster crashed onto the 100-acre field at Puttocks End. On impact in the cropped field it caught fire and exploded. Villagers also recall the presence of white lights flashing at the crossroads there, but no dummy aircraft are remembered so the existence of the decoy site remains something of a mystery.

On 8 February 1942 things were on the move again. The Accounts Section at Hyde Hall moved to Townsend House where the Equipment Section was also located, this being a more convenient location for both. Working space here was no problem for apart from the house itself 4 'Jane' huts had come from Snailwell on 20 January and been placed in the grounds as overspill accommodation.

The Battle HQ (Building 59), designed to be a defence control point in the event of the airfield being attacked by enemy forces, was abandoned on 5 March and its perimeter wire dannerts removed. In place since 15 November 1941 it was ideally positioned to suit any future airfield improvements but given up now that the threat from invasion had lessened. As a consolation, the guard room and fire party house (Building 34) and the fire tender shed (Building 35) were completed and handed over for use the same day.

Three runways at last

At the end of March the new 3-runway layout began by re-aligning the existing N–S run (no 1) onto headings of 01/19 and extending it to 1350 yards. To keep its new length in full view of the proposed watch office to be built near Shingle Hall the northern end was displaced and the rest continued southwards across the Much Hadham Road and over the fields as far as Shingle Hall. These fields, and those to the north-east, were part of the compulsory purchases necessary for the extension of the flying field. While work on this and the new 1400 yard long 06/24 runway (no 2) was in progress the '31' threshold to the north-west strip (no 3) was displaced up to Mathams Wood to enable operations to continue, albeit on a shorter run of just under 900 yards. Flying control at

BATTLE HEADQUARTERS – TYPE 11008/41
(building 59)

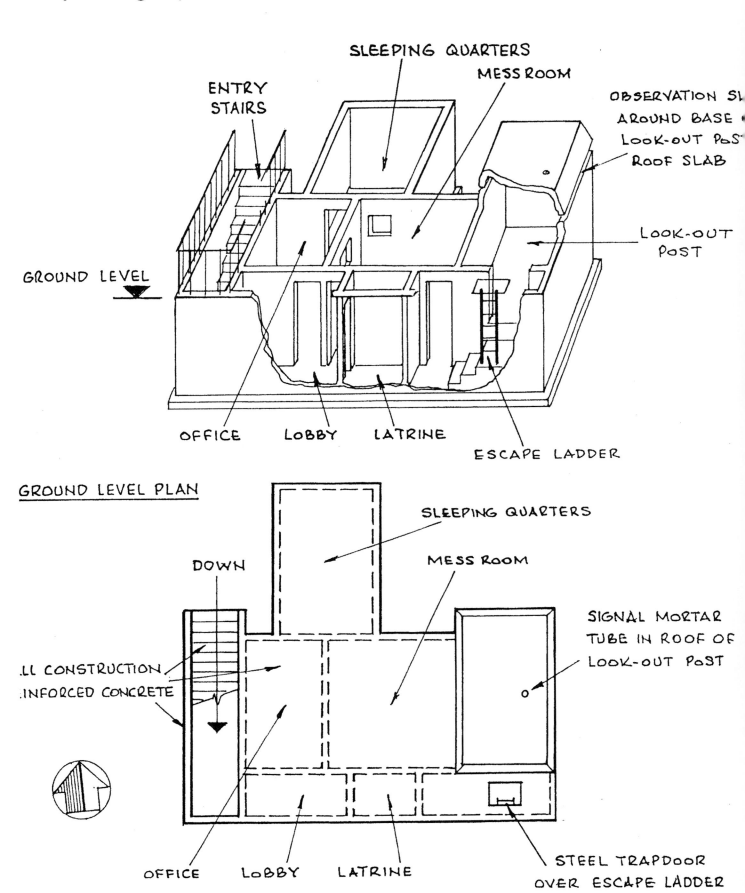

SLEEPING QUARTERS

MESS ROOM

ENTRY STAIRS

OBSERVATION SL
AROUND BASE
LOOK-OUT POS
ROOF SLAB

LOOK-OUT POST

GROUND LEVEL

OFFICE   LOBBY   LATRINE

ESCAPE LADDER

GROUND LEVEL PLAN

DOWN

SLEEPING QUARTERS

MESS ROOM

SIGNAL MORTAR TUBE IN ROOF OF LOOK-OUT POST

.LL CONSTRUCTION
.INFORCED CONCRETE

OFFICE   LOBBY   LATRINE

STEEL TRAPDOOR OVER ESCAPE LADDER

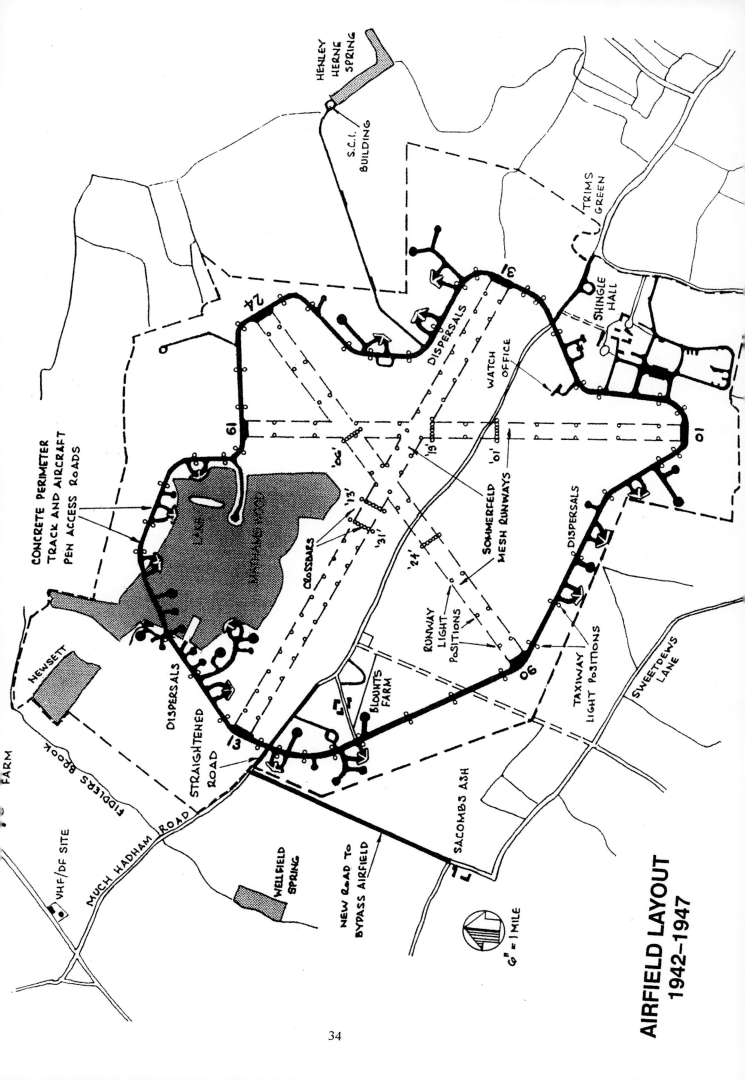

AIRFIELD LAYOUT 1942-1947

HENLEY HERNE SPRING

S.C.I. BUILDING

TRIMS GREEN

SHINGLE HALL

DISPERSALS

WATCH OFFICE

01

31

24

19

CONCRETE PERIMETER TRACK AND AIRCRAFT PEN ACCESS ROADS

CROSSBARS

'10'

'8'

'19'

'15'

'31'

'24'

SOMMERFELD MESH RUNWAYS

RUNWAY LIGHT POSITIONS

DISPERSALS

06

TAXIWAY LIGHT POSITIONS

SWEETDEWS LANE

NEWSETT

DISPERSALS

STRAIGHTENED ROAD

13

BLOUNTS FARM

SACOMBS ASH

FARM

FIDDLERS BROOK

VHF/DF SITE

MUCH HADHAM ROAD

WELLFIELD SPRING

NEW ROAD TO BYPASS AIRFIELD

6" = 1 MILE

34

this time was in the ALO briefing caravan situated near the intersection of what had been the previous two runways although the caravan was often positioned near Blounts Farm at times. The Army Air Liaison Officers had a leading hand in deciding the pattern of flying operations, this even extending to the flying carried out by the Signals Section which had a flock of homing pigeons and a mobile loft to house the birds.

Under good weather conditions approximately 1,000 yards of Sommerfeld tracking could be laid in 12 hours by 400 men. As the runways were standard width at 52 yards it required 15 rolls of track to achieve this with 75' 0" lengths being laid and tensioned in both directions before the next was laid, teams driving in steel angle-iron pickets by hand whilst bulldozers were used for straining each section. The extent of work involved can be gained by the fact that a 1,000 yard run at full width required 600 rolls of stiffened netting with 3600 connecting buckles, 3,300 steel linking plates 15' 0" long plus their joint fishplates and 2,600 pickets at a total weight of 216 tons.

All work on the runways was continuous, with the eastern half of the new 13/31 run being laid in two sections to allow operations to resume first on the 01/19 runway then on the new 06/24 direction. When these were complete in mid-April operations then transferred to the remaining half of the 13/31 runway which was relaid and extended to a new overall length of 1,700 yards. Had the need arisen, or in the event of the airfield being considered for further improvements, the runways could have been made even longer. No 1 runway (19/01) would have been extended southwards to 1,900 yards, without any relocation of the watch office, and no 2 (24/06) to 1,700 yards also to the south. The extension of no 2 would have further entailed the demolition of three houses and a cottage, plus the closure of Sacombs Ash Lane near to the junction with the private section of the road to Allens Green which was already under Air Ministry jurisdiction.

SOMMERFELD TRACKING

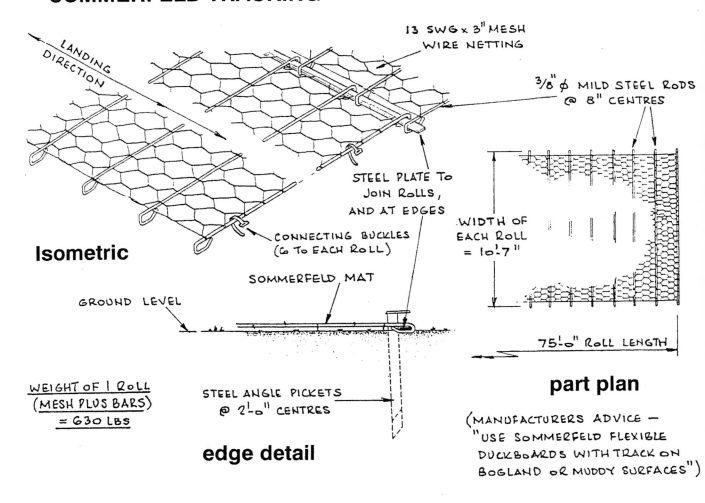

By the first week in May all three new runways were complete while the new 40' 0" wide concrete perimeter track, started at the same time, only went from Allens Green road and eastwards as far round as the two most easterly aircraft pens completed by then.

Another three months of concentrated work was necessary before the rest of the perimeter track, aircraft pens and hardstands were finished and handed over, the remaining buildings around the site not being completed until November 1942. Whereas three Over Blister hangars and eight Extended Over Blisters were placed adjacent to dispersal areas for flightline servicing only one large hangar for extended maintenance, a T2, was built at the end of 1942 on the technical site at Shingle Hall although space was available for more.

Mustangs

Whilst the airfield was being enlarged the long-awaited arrival of the aircraft that was to restructure the Army Co-operation squadrons came about with the first North American Mustangs being delivered to 2 (AC) Squadron. By comparison with the Lysander, the Allison-engined Mustang Mk 1 was a reconnaissance pilot's dream. The 1150 hp engine produced a top speed of 380 mph at 8,000 feet, although the operational height for most PR was 900, and its six-gun armament meant that it could both attack as well as defend itself.

The practice for most American fighters delivered to the UK was to send them by sea in crates to Liverpool docks, from where they were moved to nearby Speke Airport to be assembled for collection or delivery to the units. P/O J Davies collected the first Mustang Mk 1 on 19 April 1942, but on arrival at Sawbridgeworth it was confirmed that no Pilots Notes were available. While this problem was being sorted out F/Lt C F M Chapman carried out an urgent PR of Jersey that day by borrowing a Spitfire Mk 1, PR Type C, from 140 Squadron at Dyce. Four more Mustangs, plus the Pilots Notes, arrived the next day and then with six coming on 21 April familiarisation flights commenced on the type.

Initial training flights comprised all the elements of AC work; Arty/R, Tac/R, low level or message-dropping practises, and it was the latter two that contributed to the first incidents on the Mustang for 2 (AC) Squadron.

On 9 May, after only two weeks of conversion work, P/O Peter Tonkin was flying AG401 on a late morning sortie carrying out low level message dropping near Tring and in pulling up to clear a hill went through overhead electricity cables hidden below the hill. When the sparks had stopped everything seemed normal until it was realised that no airspeed was indicated, the pitot head having been torn off. On return to base the second realisation was that the radio would not work, a message dropped out over the 'A' Flight Offices being received with some amusement until his rather fast arrival confirmed its meaning. Finally, during the landing run the starboard wheel veered off into a hole under the tracking and tipped the aircraft up on its nose. Tonkin was shaken but unhurt, which is more than can be said for the pilots involved in the next traumatic incident that same day.

At around tea-time P/O G L Gosnell in AG403 was on his take-off run for a message-dropping practice when he collided with AG488 which was taxi-ing out across the adjacent grass area from dispersal. Ken Fossey, of the Signals Section Maintainence Flight, was a witness to what happened. Cycling along the Much Hadham Road from Trims Green Ken was on the airfield near 'B' Flight dispersal, when AG488 taxied out being chased by men frantically waving, as AG403 passed him from behind. At take-off speed AG403 struck AG488 with its starboard wingtip before climbing to about sixty feet, then flicked over and crashed inverted in flames near the runway. Being first on the scene Ken found the wreck still had its wheels but was minus its engine, with Gosnell outside the cockpit lying among ammunition exploding in the wreckage. He died shortly after this, his first Mustang flight, but P/O P J Willmett in AG488 was only slightly injured.

Training continued with the pilots finding out that if the Mustang was 'dropped in' when landing the tailwheel was likely to collapse, this happening on a fair number of occasions in the early days with the type. In the meantime trial installations of Rear-Facing Oblique F24 cameras were carried out

The old and the new. Comparison between men and machines by P/O Tonkin, S/L Brown, Mustang AG550 (XV–U) and Lysander T1613 (the last to serve with 2 (AC) Squadron at Sawbridgeworth).

Photo via 2 (AC) Squadron library

The F24 camera installation in its port side mounting on the Mustang shown withdrawn for servicing.

Photo via 2 (AC) Squadron library

Mustangs straining at the leash on the official press day, 24 July 1942. Nearest the camera is P/O P J Wilmett in AG636, XV–F, with P/O W R Butt in AG623, XV–W and P/O B E Hawes in AG456, XV–B of 2 (AC) Squadron. To the rear of AG636 cockpit is the open aperture which formed the F24 camera port.

'Aeroplane' photo via Chris Glynn

One man went to mow (well, daisy-cutting anyway). P/O Butt in AG623 in AC transit height. A year later at Sawbridgeworth he crashed during unauthorised aerobatics in this situation on return from an operational flight.

'Illustrated' photo via Chris Glynn

and flight-tested on 30 May. As with most American fighters the Mustang cockpit was generous enough in size to allow the F24 camera to be fitted behind the pilot and, mounted to fire out to port through an unglazed aperture on a downward incline, proved to be the best equipment for PR work as the installation allowed both servicing and film reloading to be carried out fast and easily.

More lodgers

On 6 June 2 (AC) Squadron were joined by three aircraft from 613 Squadron, two from 16 and one from 225. These part units were to participate in 'Blitz', an Arty/R exercise which ran for three days. 613 Squadron was the only ex-Auxiliary squadron to be stationed at Sawbridgeworth, the whole unit returning on 1 July 1942 for exercise 'Bury'. This ended on 4 July after seven Tac/R flights had been done, alternating between Sawbridgeworth, Snailwell and Twinwoods Farm.

On 11 July 231 Squadron sent a detached flight of Tomahawks from its Maghaberry, NI, base to join exercise 'Limpet', one of its aircraft force-landing at Sealand en route due to engine failure. Prior to taking part in 'Limpet', another Army Co-op exercise, the flight carried out local flying, then joined 2 (AC) and 268 in Tac/R work before going to Langham for the exercise proper on 14 July.

613 also took part in 'Limpet', during the course of which 20 Tac/R and five PR sorties were flown. A further seven Tac/R were flown on 16 July as the squadron moved back to Snailwell.

The power of the Press

By now fairly used to the Mk 1 Mustang, 2 (AC) Squadron was selected to show it off to the press and 24 July was picked for this event. Although airfield reconstruction work was still in progress some 50 pressmen from the aviation world were invited to the station, where they were entertained to precise demonstrations as well as formation and **very** low level flying. Charles E Brown, the celebrated photographer, who not three months before had taken in-flight shots of the Tomahawks of 2 (AC) Squadron, returned to take some of his classic studies of the Mustangs, the airborne mount for these being Battle K9277, XV–P, flown by Mustang pilot Peter Tonkin. After being used as a photo ship the Battle was borrowed by 268 Squadron to transfer personnel back to its Snailwell base, which it left for on 26 July, the Battle then being returned to 2 (AC) Squadron.

Once the press had left after the morning demonstrations, Ministry officials were given proof of the advantages the Mustang had over the Lysander, as well as controlled displays of gas and the forerunner of Napalm weapons the AC squadrons were trained to use. These were a mixture of phosphorus and benzine in reinforced 4-gallon petrol tanks fitted one to each wing strongpoint and dropped as for bombs but with grenade type fused igniters. Other types such as Hurricane and Tomahawk were also displayed, but the day marked the final appearance in AC work of the Lysander which was now firmly ear-marked for target towing, training and air/sea rescue duties in the UK. The Special Duties squadrons however still preferred it to any other type for its short-field capabilities.

Further demonstrations of AC work were given a month later when, on 25 August, low level attacks were made on the aerodrome using the resident Tiger Moth, Mustang, Master, Lysander and (would you believe) Dominie aircraft. Two days later the Mustangs were used for camouflage netting demonstrations as it had originally been intended to disperse them on the airfield in this manner but the netting was rarely, if at all, used practically.

ATC visits

The Air Training Corps was constituted by Royal Warrant on 5 February 1941 as the successor to the peace-time Air Defence Cadet Corps formed on 7 April 1938 under Air League instructions. The intention was to promote and encourage young men to take a practical interest in aviation and fit them to serve their country; it was also a prerequisite for joining the RAF and hundreds of entrants came from this source. Part of the training programme included visits to active establishments throughout the war and Sawbridgeworth was no exception.

Visits to the station were slightly different to others in terms of the luxuries afforded, particularly when compared with nearby Stansted where the cadets had the free run of far too many facilities. At Sawbridgeworth the visitors were crammed into the wooden huts at Shingle Hall where meals were taken and lectures given on engines, weapons or other technical matters. On a practical vein associated with the operational side of life they were given 'glamour' jobs such as washing vehicles, but not aircraft, before reaping the benefits of their labours by getting the flying they expected.

Up to the end of 1941 flights were given in Lysanders, but in 1942 (the last year recorded as seeing ATC visits) the majority were done in Tiger Moths with the odd use of the de Havilland Dominie and Miles Master aircraft. All these were flown off the early tracked runway to the north side of the Much Hadham Road with cadets based at the guard hut and emergency services sheds near to the private Allens Green road. Peter Brown (ex 1096 Squadron ATC) recalls that from here in late 1941 the Tomahawk dispersals to the east and those for Lysanders to the south of Mathams Wood could be seen.

Peter Tonkin joined 2 (AC) Squadron in April 1942 to fly Tomahawks, and later Mustangs, but for the rest of that year held the post of ATC officer. This involved the co-ordination of visits and the provision of flying facilities, much non-operational flying time being gained in this capacity on Oxfords and Proctors also. The job also required Peter to fly visiting pressmen around, such as when the Mustang was introduced to the press on 24 July, generally in one of the Fairey Battles retained after the AC tests.

Other Liaisons

On 13 September 1942 the Fleet Air Arm arrived in the shape of 3 Fairey Fulmars on detachment for army co-operation practices. Three days later they, along with six aircraft from 'A' flight, 2 (AC) Squadron, operated from RAF Honington and participated in Exercise 'Bull'. They left on 19 September but on 30 September a further flight of 6 Fulmars from 809 Squadron FAA left RNAS St Mawgan in Cornwall and arrived for a two-week stay on similar duties. Once again attached to 2 (AC) Squadron the flight was to learn the trade of army co-operation prior to participating in Operation 'Torch', the North Africa landings. This squadron was not new to the area as some of its members had visited the station in May and been given familiarisation flights in Tiger Moths of 2 (AC) Squadron. Over the period of this later stay the 12 officers (billetted at Hyde Hall) were assisted by their own ground crews in the form of 54 ratings (billetted on the airfield) and carried out artillery co-operation and message-dropping, the latter being practised using the marked field to the north of Blounts Farm as the target zone. Tactical reconnaissance flying at very low level was also practised, with the Naval observers being trained to use the F24 camera in a hand-held situation.

Whilst at Sawbridgeworth the detachment, formed from 879 Squadron FAA as 'B' flight of 809 on 1 October, carried out the initial FAA trials with the Napalm weapons, 'blaze bombs', which were intended for use in North Africa. As they were still considered a dangerous weapon live stores were not used in practice drops, water-filled ones being used instead. Additionally, on 6 October, five of the Fulmars accompanied 8 Mustangs in an air-to-ground firing demonstration on the Potters Bridge ranges near Colliers End on the A10.

When 809 departed on 11 October it was to RNAS Macrihanish on the (frozen) west coast of Scotland for an intensive deck-landing course before re-embarking on the carrier HMS Victorious. On the carrier their blaze bombs were stored in the relatively safe area of the flight deck round-down but due to no enemy opposition in Algiers, the intended area of operations, they were not used in anger.

Major Noel East (late of the East Kent Regiment, but like most AILOs seconded to the RAF from the Army) briefs P/Os Hawes and Wilmett outside the mobile Intelligence caravan at Blounts Farm prior to their carrying out a Mustang pair flying session on 24 July 1942.

Four days after this picture was taken Brian Hawes was killed flying in Mustang AG478 which crashed on a cross-country flight near Penzance. Wing Commander Peter Riddell, OC 2 (AC) Squadron, seen here seated next to message-dropping containers and a non-digital field telephone, won screen fame as the Intelligence Officer in the classic RAF wartime epic *Target for Tonight*. *Photo via 2 (AC) Squadron library*

Amongst these 809 Squadron Fulmers ranged on the deck of HMS Victorious in September 1942 are those that detached to Sawbridgeworth for exercises the following month. *R C Sturtivant photo*

A brute of a plane, the Typhoon Mk 1b, operated by 182 Squadron from Sawbridgeworth to work up for attacks on coastal radar stations and other tactical targets.

Stormy weather

With the airfield to themselves once again 2 (AC) Squadron continued its conversion onto the Mustang but 29 October was to be a disastrous day. Three aircraft were despatched on a training flight only to run into bad weather, which had worsened by the time they returned to base.

After one hour the formation became lost whilst trying to locate the airfield and flew northwards from Stanstead Abbots until they were forced down due to low cloud, and at 150' above local ground level the right-hand Mustang AG605, XV-A, flown by P/O D B Williams, hit the edge of Easenye Woods. The remaining aircraft broke away under the low cloudbase, P/O P W Leah in AG633, 'E', eventually found the airfield but made a wheels-up landing whilst P/O P M Gordon-Crosby in AG456, 'B', turned west to find better weather. After a total of 2½ hrs flying in horrific conditions he abandoned his aircraft over Ludgershall, Buckinghamshire, the demise of all three being agreed at the Court of Inquiry held on 31 October as due once again mainly to failure of the aircraft wireless sets in not being able to make contact with base for a homing.

The crash of AG605 was witnessed by Leslie Miller, then a schoolboy living in Stanstead Abbots. At the time he found some fittings from the aircraft and, although it had been cleared by the military, searched the site some years later to find more. In the course of preparing this book it was decided to investigate the crash site more thoroughly as it had lain undisturbed since 1942 and considered a relevent part of the airfield history. It was also considered to be a most significant incident relating to a Sawbridgeworth-based unit as the pilot was of extremely high calibre.

Pilot Officer Derek Bell Williams was the second son of five children to a noted Liverpool Councillor and solicitor. An all-round sportsman, he was an old boy of Birkenhead School where he had been in the first cricket XI and rugby teams, and by the start of the Second World War was studying for a business career and in the Territorials. He transferred to the RAF where he was a brilliant cadet, heading the list at most examinations, and after passing out took his commission and joined 2 (AC) Squadron. After a period of exemplary service he was offered an instructing post nearer to his home town but declined as he preferred to stay with the squadron. Aged 26, he was killed when his aircraft broke up completely upon impact with the trees at Easenye, his body being brought down from the treetops by Ware Fire Brigade and returned to his native town for burial. His funeral on 2 November 1942 commenced with a memorial service in the chapel at Birkenhead School, before interment in the cemetery at nearby Landican, members of 2 (AC) Squadron being in attendance.

Investigation of the crash site in 1995 followed the approvals of landowner and MoD being given. The author, his son and Leslie Miller swept the crash site after first positioning the items previously found near the initial impact point, a mutilated tree now recently felled. In roughly a 100' 0" long crescent-shaped area were found the dial from the engine RPM gauge, various pipe fittings, one set of rear fuselage oxygen bottles, a smashed D/V sliding window, cell dividers from the aircraft batteries and portions of radio. After a lunch break and discussion of tactics, the end of the search area revealed parts of the main fuselage structure, brake disc and wheel bearing races, fragments of gearbox castings and exploded 0.5" calibre gun ammunition, along with a 1934 penny. No large portions were discovered, all these having been cleared some 53 years previously, but the many items recovered all displayed intense fragmentation and testified to the severity of the crash of this Mustang which never quite made it home.

Nearly finished

By the end of October 1942 many official visits had been made to the station, it by now having most of its Blister hangars and other buildings and being virtually complete. The NAAFI opened up on the Communal Site to provide sustenance for the ORs, and the new WAAF site was finished in time for the 120-strong contingent to move in by 4 December.

2 (AC) Squadron completed its conversion training and was deemed operational on the Mk 1 Mustang on 14 November when S/L Houseman and F/Lt Kenning carried out a PR of the RDF

Both sides of an RAF Form 1180, the 'crash card', in this case that of 2 (AC) Squadron Mustang AG605. Note that Sawbridgeworth has not been given as the aircraft's home drome, and that the card has been overwritten 'wireless' as the main cause of the accident. *RAF Museum*

Wartime shot looking south-east. Across the fields in the background is Shingle Hall with Mathams Wood on the left and runway 13/31 to the right of it. The road changes at Blounts Farm are visible whilst across the foreground, literally where the photo frame numbers are, is the line of the Lancaster force-landing in March 1944.

RAF Museum photo

A VHF/DF hut, with its aerials, similar to that built outside the western boundary at Sawbridge-worth.

This type was erected at Juvencourt, France after D–day and clad in fabric to cut down transport weight.

Ernest Tomlinson photo

The guardroom at Shingle Hall now serves as offices, with the nearby fire tender shed a store.
Paul Francis photo, 1984

The 343/43 pattern watch office was demolished without any photos being taken of it. This pristine example of similar type is at Little Walden, Cambs.

station at Domburg on the island of Walcheren, Holland. The flight was uneventful but due to low cloud the sortie, an oblique line overlap, was made from 350 feet and the resulting photographs useless so a return visit at 1,000 feet was made four days later.

After the process of getting pilots 'operational' on the Mustang had finished the type was not without its problems in respect of recognition by friendly fighters and AA guns. Being a new shape in the sky and bearing a close resemblance to the German Me 109 it was in more danger of being lost due to friendly fire, as was the Blenheim in 1940 when wrongly mis-identified as the Junkers Ju 88. The Typhoon entered service in 1941 and it was found that, under certain conditions, it could be mistaken for the Focke Wulf FW 190 and initial recognition measures included painting the nose section white. The Mustang also had vivid markings added, consisting of 9" wide yellow identity bands painted chordwise around both wings, outboard of the gun positions. For a short period Typhoons also carried such markings until they were removed from both types after a long enough period had elapsed for everyone to know the difference between new Allied and German aircraft.

Although by now phased out of front line service some squadrons still had Tomahawks on strength, 2 (AC) being one. The last incident at Sawbridgeworth involving a Tomahawk of this unit was on 25 November 1942 when P/O P M Gordon-Crosby stalled AK144 on the approach after setting the mixture control instead of the propellor pitch. The result was that the engine failed and the aircraft spun in, no disciplinary action being taken against Gordon-Crosby as it was considered that his injuries were sufficient punishment.

The end of 1942 saw further changes around the station with the Station HQ moving to Shingle Hall, whilst 2 (AC) Squadron HQ and the AIL section went into new offices in Blounts Farm, on 3 December. On 15 December Great Hyde Hall was handed over to 211 MU as the base for its equipment issuing role and Wing Commander Bristow arrived that day as the new Station Commander.

2 (AC) Squadron went to Martlesham Heath on 5 December for 'Scorch', a two-day exercise, and when it returned its Mustangs led in the 17 Typhoons and a Hurricane of 182 Squadron. 182 was the only unit to operate the heavy Mk 1b Typhoon from Sawbridgeworth but, due to the usual problems with mud on the dispersal areas, both 2 (AC) and 182 Squadrons initially sent six aircraft to Hunsdon for flying training whilst more mesh was laid at dispersals.

When operating in the 'Bomphoon' role the Typhoon, already mounting four 20mm cannon, carried a 250-pounder under each wing which increased its all-up weight to 12,250 lbs. In this configuration it tended to lift its tail and 'buck' on take-off from the grassed or tracked surfaces, however no accidents occurred in training and two aircraft eventually carried out the squadron's first (and only) offensive operation from Sawbridgeworth to Bruges on 3 January 1943.

The watch office (control tower) and its three ancillary buildings for fire engine shed, night flying equipment store and floodlight trailer/tractor shed were finally finished, as was the signals square with its two-letter airfield identity code of 'ZH' for day use only. With only the sole T2 hangar remaining to be completed on the technical site at Shingle Hall, and the N–S runway mesh relaid due to wear in the touch-down areas, on 30 December 1942 the airfield site had now increased to 615 acres.

That same day the last Fairey Battle accident occurred on the station and was of a major but rather embarrassing nature. P/O Peter Tonkin of 2 (AC) Squadron was taxi-ing K9277 across the airfield when the tail fell off in going over rough ground. Fatigue and corrosion had affected the rivets and the whole tail section came away, but no blame was due to anyone as the aircraft was over four years old and had seen service with three other units before coming to 2 (AC) Squadron.

New Year changes

On 17 January 1943 182 Squadron sent 14 aircraft (ten from Sawbridgeworth and four from Hunsdon) in formation to Snailwell for further training, returning on 20 January, but in order for the whole squadron to fly together more frequent detachments were made to Hunsdon. When the Station

WATCH OFFICE – 12779/41
(building 7)

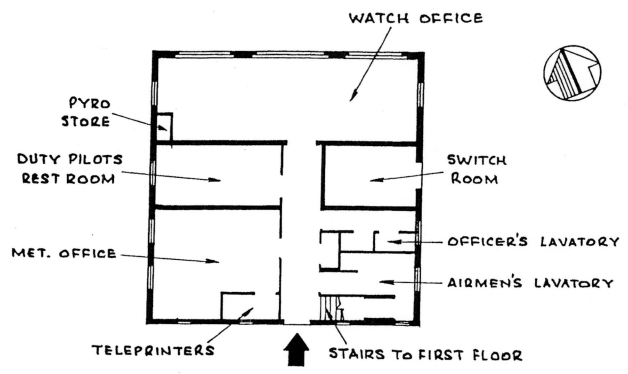

WATCH OFFICE

PYRO STORE

DUTY PILOTS REST ROOM

SWITCH ROOM

MET. OFFICE

OFFICER'S LAVATORY

AIRMEN'S LAVATORY

TELEPRINTERS

STAIRS TO FIRST FLOOR

GROUND FLOOR PLAN

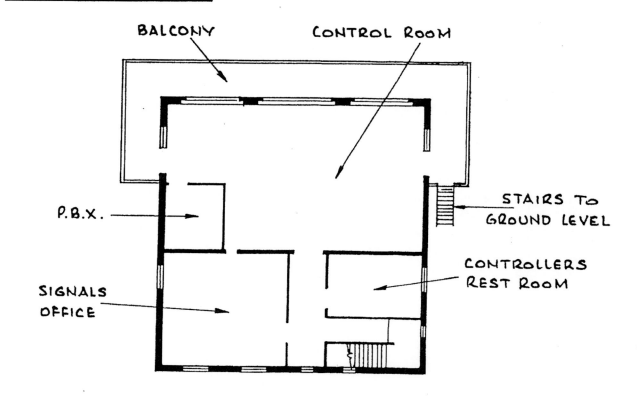

BALCONY

CONTROL ROOM

P.B.X.

STAIRS TO GROUND LEVEL

CONTROLLERS REST ROOM

SIGNALS OFFICE

FIRST FLOOR PLAN

Commander declared the runways unserviceable due to flooding after heavy rain on 22 January 182 Squadron busied itself with dinghy drills and range firing practice for the following week. After a visit by Air Marshal Sir Arthur Barratt, AOC of Army Co-operation Command, it was stated that the squadron had to be moved to better facilities for training to be completed and 182 then left for Martlesham Heath on 30 January, after a month when many operations were not possible due to the airfield being frequently unserviceable due to flooding and mud on the dispersal areas.

2 (AC) left for Bottisham the same day and it was the first in a series of occasions when no squadrons were on the station from the time of its establishment in 1940. Ironically it was also the day for the arrival of a unit raised specifically to deal with aircraft, this being 3226 Servicing Commando Unit. Its function was to service and defend combat aircraft on landing grounds recently occupied from the enemy, one of the many mobile support units formed in August 1942 with the invasion of mainland Europe in mind. Without any actual aircraft to work on it concentrated on ground training until it left in April.

The 'empty' period ended in February when the aircraft of 652 Squadron arrived en masse from Dumfries after exercise 'Spartan', the largest tactical exercise carried out thus far in the UK. The unit, flying the little Cirrus Minor-powered Taylorcraft Auster Mk 1 and commanded by Major R M Coble of the Royal Artillery, served in the air observation post (AOP) role and during Spartan had operated from temporary steel-mesh tracked LGs put down by 13 ACG at Red Barn and Eastmanton Down, Berkshire. Accommodation was sorted out on 17 February and the squadron moved in officially on the 21st when Blounts Farm was taken over as HQ, the ground staff being given various training lectures until the Auster Mk 1s of 'C' flight came on the 28th.

It was during this period of stay by 652 Squadron that a photo sortie was made of the airfield in a Magister to check on the aspects of camouflage, but the photos taken on 11 March show no trace of any Austers, so good was their dispersal technique. The rest of the aircraft arrived on 12 March, then re-equipment with the Gipsy Major-powered Mk 3 followed on the 18th when 12 aircraft arrived and training continued in order to further the squadron's use in the AOP/AC role. Due to its relatively low weight and landing speed the Austers coped well with inclement weather and the steel mat runways, both of which had proved a problem to faster and heavier types, and during its short stay the squadron received 17 of the Mk 1 and 18 Mk 3 which were operated very successfully.

23 March however proved to be a bad day, when two Mk 3s were lost in two separate training sorties. Auster MZ139 crashed and caught fire near Little Hormead during an Arty/R practice, badly burning the pilot, whilst MZ161 crashed and burnt in the course of a fighter evasion exercise near Furneaux Pelham. The Auster was being pursued by a Mosquito and in order to escape flew down a valley. Unfortunately the pilot was too intent on watching his pursuer for during the course of a steep turn below tree-top height he flew into the rising ground. Again the Army captain pilot was burnt but survived whereas the aircraft, delivered that very day, was destroyed.

One week later, on 30 March, the remainder of 652 Squadron's aircraft took off and left in formation for their new base at Almondbank (Perth).

In March the station received as its satellite Stapleford Tawney, Essex, which had just been transferred to 34 Wing Army Co-operation Command. It was grass-surfaced and remained so throughout the war. Upon disbandment of 34 Wing in June it transferred to No 12 Group but remained Sawbridgeworth's satellite as a back-up to the preparations involved in the formation of the Second Tactical Air Force which were finalised on 15 November 1943. Little use however was made of Stapleford, either for training, exercises or as a diversion airfield but it remained available if required.

Another of the 'unusual' lodgers arrived in mid-May for a two-month stay, this being 1495 (TT) Flight with its Lysander 2 and Miles Martinet 1 aircraft. A touring unit that provided target-towing facilities for air-to-air firing practices it was classified as a Co-operation Squadron and fitted in well at Sawbridgeworth where it served 2 (AC) Squadron.

Low-level losses

Although 2 (AC) Squadron tended to treat Sawbridgeworth as its home station, indeed it spent most of its WW2 time there and more than any other unit posted in, it was of course sent to other bases for exercises or as dictated by operational needs. It was on one such detachment during its second stay of 1943 that it suffered its worst losses on any single operation.

Having returned to Sawbridgeworth on 27 April it was sent to Thruxton in late May with 12 Mustangs and a Dominie support aircraft for an intended mass Ranger operation named 'Asphalt'. On arrival there the squadron had to endure two postponements due to bad weather over the Channel but, on 26 May, the operation was 'on'. F/Lt George Kenning took off in charge of 10 aircraft at 1645 hours, the brief being to attack rail targets in the area bounded by Rennes-Laval-Le Mans-Chateau Briant-Blain-Redon-Rennes, but the weather worsened and Kenning rightly brought the formation home. Flying out of France in line abreast height had to be reduced progressively until sea level flight was attained over the Channel.

On reaching the Dorset coast in the Kimmeridge/St Albans Head area a dense wall of sea fog was met and Kenning gave the order to climb out through it, but unfortunately Flying Officers N J Miller (in AG550, XV-U), D Hurst (AG623, 'W') and J B McLeod (AP210, 'Y') did not respond and crashed into the fog-covered St Albans Head. The rest of the formation orbited their last known position but the missing aircraft were not found. Ground searches later confirmed their worst fears.

On return to Thruxton, where Flying Officer M P Dunkerley (XV–N) returned late with a total hydraulic failure, operations were officially abandoned at 1735 hours due to bad weather but this did not help appease the feelings of the pilots who returned to Sawbridgeworth two days later to relate with regret the hazards of low level sweep operations.

The latter days

At the end of May 1943 Sawbridgeworth ceased to be controlled by Army Co-operation Command and, on 1 June, Fighter Command officially took charge. That the value of the airfield was appreciated by its new owners can be gauged by the fact that over the next two months, until it was first 'officially' put onto C & M, no Fighter Command units were based at, or operated from, the station. The nearest that true fighters ever got to taking an interest in it was when a Spitfire 9, EE253, flown by Sgt J M Ritchie of 19 Squadron came to grief on 10 June during a non-operational cross-country flight. For reasons unknown tree foliage had blocked the radiator air entry and a forced landing was made west of the Much Hadham Road. The pilot was uninjured but brought to the SSQ for a check-up.

30 June saw 2759 Squadron RAF Regiment move in from Stapleford Tawney for a two-week stay. It was a Field Squadron of 7 officers and 178 airmen, comprising a HQ flight, three rifle flights, an armoured car flight and a support flight. The term 'rifle' flight disguised the true facts that these comprised one flight each of rifle, 3" mortar and Vickers light machine-gun. In the early days of the RAFR the armoured car flights had used the well-known Beaverette but changed to the Humber 4x4 in 1943. 2759 barely had time to take part in anything but perimeter defence before it moved out to Snailwell on 13 July.

July saw four more incidents involving Mustangs of 2 (AC) Squadron prior to their leaving the station. F/O W Redman in AG539 landed with tailwheel retracted on the 1st, F/O W R Butt was killed in AP220 on the 5th when he beat up the airfield on return from a long operational flight and crashed during a series of low rolls, F/Lt W Shepheard in AM234 landed in formation on the 8th but caught the leader's slipstream and put a wing into the ground, and F/O S J Shayle-George in AG541 did the same on the 10th except that his undercarriage collapsed in the resulting swing and the aircraft ended up off the runway on its nose.

Notwithstanding these events a 2 (AC) Squadron party was held in the Communal Site Officers' Mess on 3 July, this being the last function before they moved to Gravesend on 16 July in two more

Townsend House on London Road. In 1940 it was one of the town properties requisitioned for Air Force use as the Equipment Section but is now office accommodation.

Apart from the ubiquitous Nissen many other hutting types were built. This is the asbestos-clad Handcraft at the rear of Bursteads.

51

Although the roof has been modified the Parachute Store (Building 14) at Shingle Hall still shows traces of its ancestry. *Photo: Paul Francis, 1984*

The ambulance garage (Building 7), denoted by its large door opening, also served for a while as the mortuary on the Station Sick Quarters Site but is now a vehicle workshop on the Clarklands Industrial Estate.

parties, air and ground. The current airfield guard unit, 2759 RAFR, in moving to Snailwell on 13 July made their move in true military style of four ground parties (advance, rear, cycle and road).

For the next four months no aircraft operated from the airfield but, reduced once again to C & M status on 7 August and at the same time transferred from No 12 to No 11 Group, the only aircraft movement was a Handley Page Harrow of 271 Squadron which landed on 15 August to collect stores from 211 MU at Great Hyde Hall.

Various operational orders then began flying about. On 19 August information was received that 410 R & SU (Repair and Salvage Unit) was to be formed on the station instead of at West Malling on 1 September. 15 September brought news that that nos 53 and 54 Mobile Field Hospitals, plus nos 3 and 4 Casualty Air Evacuation Units, were to be formed on 23 September, and the arrival on 5 October of officers from the unit gave two days' notice that 2876 Squadron of the RAF Regiment would be arriving. For a station placed on C & M the sudden inrush of newly-formed units meant that peace and quiet did not return to the once-muddy fields, in fact quite a fair number of hob-nailed boots were still very much in evidence.

When 410 R & SU arrived facilities on the Communal Site were available, but not a stick of furniture was to be seen. This, according to the unit ORB, was rectified on 5 September when enough furniture and stationery was obtained from other units and the SHQ by persuasion and organised theft to start the unit off. The R & SU was supposed to retrieve crashed or war-weary aircraft of either side for repair or reducing to produce, but most of the time spent at Sawbridgeworth was taken up with dances or film shows in the Gym or the minor matter of battlefield training. On 23 October Nos 2 and 3 Repair Parties went to Biggin Hill to join 403 R & SU whilst the remainder of the unit moved out to Detling on 30 November.

The Mobile Field Hospitals, and their associated Casualty Air Evacuation Units, were just as the name implied. They would move up behind advancing troops in order to provide close medical care, but in the event of injuries requiring more precise hospital attention the CAEU would organise despatch of the casualties direct to mainland Britain.

To give an idea of the personnel involved in just one unit the staffing levels for 53 MFH/3 CAEU are given:

- ❏ Commanding Officer (of Wing Commander rank) plus deputy of Squadron Leader rank
- ❏ Air Liaison Section, comprising 6 Sgts, 8 Cpls and 33 Airmen
- ❏ Medical Section, comprising 5 officers, 11 aircraft hands, 1 carpenter, 2 chemical warfare fighters, 4 clerks, 3 cooks, 17 drivers, 1 equipment assistant, 1 electrician, 4 MT fitters and mechanics, 28 medical staff, 2 motor cyclists and one specialised hospital cook.

This shows a total of 258 persons for the two hospitals, plus 48 for the R & SU and 370 for the RAF Regiment, whilst not forgetting 211 MU which had been at nearby Hyde Hall since December 1942 with its complement of 125; it can therefore be seen that over 800 persons were still on or near the station at this time in addition to the necessary guard and fire/ emergency services.

53 MFH arrived on 23 September, and 54 MFH on the 26th when S/L T C Davies from 121 Airfield officially opened up both units. Initially officers billets were at Shingle Hall whilst the senior NCOs used cottages at nearby Trims Green and other ranks occupied tents erected in the field behind the easterly dispersals, but when the Commanding Officer, W/C H F Harvey, arrived on 4 October he had both MFHs re-accommodated in the better facilities at Blounts Farm. This was coincident with the British School of Motoring coming for a week to train all the spare drivers up to the standard required.

On 10 November 53 and 54 MFHs left for Snailwell in a convoy of 72 vehicles (28 for each MFH and 8 each for the two CAEUs), taking two and a half hours for this veritable snake to cover the 40-mile journey over not exactly the best of English roads. After spending the winter of 1943/44 in quarters near Snailwell both the MFHs and the CAEUs then progressed via intermediate bases to transit camps in the New Forest area. They then awaited their turn to move to the Continent to provide the advancing armies with medical facilities.

In the meantime 2876 Sqn RAFR had arrived on 7 October, with the addition of 2809 on 15 October, supposedly for winter quartering. 2809 had formed in 1941 as 809 defence squadron but became a light AA unit in May 1943, 2876 forming as an AA unit in July.

Apart from taking post on anti-aircraft duties both squadrons carried out rifle training and aircraft recognition, the latter still sadly lacking in proficiency as many RAF pilots found out to their cost. 2876 left on 10 November for the Regimental depot at Grantham whilst 2809 took the now-familiar route to Snailwell on 15 November.

Flying units then returned and from November 1943 to March 1944. It was another busy period at Sawbridgeworth for, apart from the 'resident' 2 (AC) Squadron, five other operational squadrons were based there with various types of aircraft. On 12 November the station (still on C & M) reverberated to the throb of aero engines once more when 123 Airfield's three Mustang-equipped squadrons 63, 168 and 170 moved in from Thruxton. Their stay began with 63 bringing in 20 Mk 1a plus a Master 3, then 168 and 170 arrived that afternoon in one large formation with their Mustangs. 63 started off with pair flying, plus 'Lagoon' and 'Popular' sorties (a total of 83 from Sawbridgeworth) but by the end of the month all three units were on Anti-Rhubarb sorties along the French and Dutch coasts, weather permitting.

Although a lot of aircraft sustained hits from coastal flak or were damaged flying through trees on low pair flying exercises combat losses by now had reduced significantly, but on 24 November one of the 170 Squadron Mustangs, FD483, was lost during the course of a local training flight. The aircraft crashed onto the Much Hadham Road south of 'Whitehall', just west of Bishops Stortford, and caught fire with the pilot, F/O Hector W Munro, being killed.

This had been the only training flight that day, other aircraft of 63 and 170 Squadrons being on 'Bodyline' sorties to France and 'Lagoons' to the Dutch coast whilst 63 and 168 also covered artillery shoots at Docking and Eastbourne. After this the Sawbridgeworth weather again got the better of things with frequent cancellations of PR ops either due to fog or the airfield being so deep in mud that aircraft movements were impossible.

On 30 November 63 and 168 moved out to North Weald, to be replaced by 2 (AC) and 4 Squadrons who moved in from North Weald later that same day. 170 Squadron remained on site for a few months more, carrying out Link Trainer work and seconding 'A' Flight to the PRU at Benson for the occasional Noball sortie, until it was disbanded on 15 January 1944.

4 Squadron was a low-level PR unit operating the Mustang 1. When it arrived with 2 (AC) Squadron from North Weald it had only five servicable aircraft, but settled in and began local flying the next day. Due to fog and the usual problem of mud the airfield was deemed u/s except for four Lagoons which used the one good weather slot on 5 December, but generally no flying was possible from 2–9 December. On this last day the crews were given sunbed treatment and dental inspections, but by mid-day on 10 December the weather had cleared and all five Mustangs were ordered off on shipping recces along the Dutch coast, one landing back immediately with engine failure. The rest of the pilots went to Hunsdon where a Mosquito T3 was made available for conversion training, this new type being expected on the squadron in the New Year, when its role would change to that of high level PR.

On 12 December four Mustang Lagoon sorties managed to be flown but for the rest of the month frost and snow precluded any further useful operations. More Mosquito conversion work was carried out on the T3 at Hunsdon and at the end of the year only two Mustangs were on strength, the rest having been loaned to 2 and 170 Squadrons.

On New Year's Day 1944 Spitfire PR11s were issued to 4 Squadron to provide single-seat, low altitude capability and, along with the Mosquito T3, flew training flights from Hunsdon before a move was made to Aston Down the next day to collect the promised Mosquitoes which were of the PR 16 type. With the variety of aircraft types on strength it had been anticipated that the squadron could then operate as a high/low level PR and Tac/R unit but, as events turned out, the use of the Mosquito alone would fulfil all these tasks.

2 (AC) Squadron carried on with low-level Tac/R work until 22 January when it moved to North Weald, but sent detached flights to Benson to help the PRU catch up with its workload which had been assisted previously by 170 Squadron, and with no resident aircraft on the station it was left to a solitary unknown Spitfire to keep the fire and crash crews occupied. On 28 January the aircraft force-landed on the trackway with minor mechanical problems, but the pilot was uninjured and the aircraft sent on its way soon afterwards.

2 (AC) Squadron returned on 29 February with 20 Mustangs as the advance party of 35 (Recce) Wing of 2nd TAF to await the return of 4 and 268, all three units being unable to form up as 130 Airfield at North Weald due to lack of space there. The main party in the form of 268 Squadron's 20 Mustangs arrived on 1 March being, with 2 (AC), the low-level elements.

The high-level element in the form of 4 Squadron arrived on 3 March in a grand formation of four Spitfires leading six Mosquitoes, with eight more Spitfires and four Mustangs behind, but this impressive collection of types in one unit failed to impress the weather which caused the cancellation of many sorties for the rest of the month. The Wing HQ had been present for some time, having set up winter quarters the previous autumn, the senior RAF Intelligence Officer being Laurence Irving, grandson of the Victorian actor Henry Irving.

Aircraft maintenance methods had changed by now. Previously pilots had used a particular aircraft which had its own ground crew, but this changed when servicing was carried out on a central basis. 6268 Servicing Echelon, based on the technical site, did the routine checks and necessary repairs before issuing the aircraft back to its unit. This now meant that pilots did not have their 'own' aircraft, but merely used the next available which had its own limited flight line crew.

Operating the heavy Mosquito off the Sommerfeld tracking proved to be a problem for 'B' Flight of 4 Squadron. After navigation training sorties on 6 March it was found that stones from beneath the tracking, loosened by the wheels and flung up by prop-wash, had badly damaged the tailplanes on all six aircraft and rendered them 'u/s'. That same day G/C P L Donkin, OC 35 Wing, took an 'A' Flight Spitfire on an unspecified flight over Holland. He did the same on 8 March but details of the sorties have not come to light.

7 March saw a Spitfire carry out 4 Squadron's first official operation since its last stay in December 1943 when a PR was made of V1 launch sites on the French coast, but full cloud cover over the target area rendered the mission a failure. The off-the-job Mosquito observers from 'B' Flight meanwhile used Tiger Moths for low level map reading practice.

On 8 March the weather improved significantly such that three Spitfire PR sorties of French and Dutch airfields, plus training sorties, were successfully carried out.

Meanwhile 2 (AC) Squadron went to Dundonald on 11 March for a course in spotting the fall of shot of Naval bombardment, as a precursor to the Normandy landings which were getting nearer all the time although the exact date was still not notified. It returned on 25 March when 268 Squadron went to Dundonald for the same purpose.

PR of Dutch airfields was the role throughout March for the Spitfires of 'A' Flight, 4 Squadron, whilst the Mosquitoes of 'B' Flight were returned to serviceability. The Mosquitoes had been tasked to do a mosaic of Kings Lynn-Colchester-Hemel Hempstead for the Army before the end of the month but bad weather again precluded this on 13 March when all five aircraft aborted, although the Spitfires managed to perform their tasks with moderate success.

During this no-flying spell much Link Trainer practice was gained, also communications duties with the Magister and Auster types, but the morale of 268 Squadron was affected to such a degree by the adverse weather stopping operational sorties for its pilots to demand weather check flights be flown, forecasts having been 100% wrong during the last weeks.

The first successful Mosquito PR by 4 Squadron was carried out on 20 March when MM313 'T' covered Twente airfield in Holland, while the Spitfires switched over to Noball recces, but on 22 March the squadron's luck changed again. With all its Mosquitoes again airworthy, 'B' Flight lost an aircraft when MM309 'R' crashed during its take-off run for a training flight. After swinging uncontrollably in both directions the undercarriage collapsed and the aircraft was extensively damaged, but no fire ensued and both crew members were luckily uninjured. It says a lot for the Mosquito construction that, after repair in the works of Martin Hearn Ltd, MM309 returned to 4 Squadron service early in 1945.

PR sorties for 4 Squadron Spitfires were more plentiful than the Mustangs or Mosquitoes during March, with 37 at low level against the Mustangs 15, and only 7 high level Mosquito of which three were aborted over the target area due to cloud cover. By 30 March the requested mosaics still had not been done, and although four Spitfires and a Mosquito were on standby every day the bad weather took charge. An earlier recce of Gatwick had found it to be available and have good weather for longer periods and, as the pre D-Day photo coverage was now taking priority, the whole of 35 Wing moved there on 4 April.

A much larger, and more desperate, visitor arrived on the evening of 31 March. On return from a raid on Nuremburg a 514 Squadron Lancaster encountered fog around Waterbeach, its home base. After much time had been spent trying to get into several diversion fields petrol ran so low that three of the crew were baled out and a crash landing made with undercarriage up over Newsett onto the western grass area. The aircraft however ran on across the Much Hadham Road, passed between Blounts and Wellfield Spring, then crossed Brook Lane before finally coming to a halt in a field west of Sacombs Ash. After this long and interesting ground run the pilot, W/O McGowan, and the rest of his crew were uninjured, the aircraft being dismantled by 70 MU and removed by road two days later.

Although the airfield was (technically) put on C & M on 7 August 1943 many units were still using it for operations and/or training. When 2 (AC) Squadron left for the last time on 4 April 1944, going to Gatwick with 4 and 268 as 35 Wing, the landing areas were declared fit for emergency use only and airfield services run down. Three weeks later the next flying unit moved in . . .

No 80 Squadron had returned to the UK from the Mediterranean area, where Spitfire 5c were used, for re-equipment with the Spitfire 9b but no aircraft arrived with the aircrews. The entire squadron had travelled from Naples by sea on HMTS Almanzora and disembarked at Glasgow docks, then used special trains to get to Sawbridgeworth where they arrived at 0400 hrs on 24 April. Catering staff provided a very early breakfast for them. Immediately all personnel were given embarkation leave, then the following day their kit arrived. Over the course of the next five days the aircraft began to appear, but these turned out to be a mixture of Mks 5c and 9 instead of the Spitfire 9b expected.

On 30 April 126 Squadron arrived, this had served in Malta and Italy and was also to receive new Spitfire 9b before working up alongside 80 Squadron and then move on, 126 to go to RAF Culmhead at the end of this posting and 80 Squadron to join 229 & 274 in a new wing at RAF Hornchurch.

To cope with the sudden requirement for aviation fuel, stocks had to be brought in. This was dealt with by a 42 Group detachment served by 211 MU at Hyde Hall, but until the stocks of jerry-cans arrived on 1 May no operations were carried out.

Meanwhile postings-in continued, whilst those on embarkation leave returned to their new station. On 5 May, having got its full quota, the pilots of 80 Squadron moved to Hornchurch whilst 18 new Spitfire 9b arrived for 126 Squadron.

6 May saw the rest of 80 Squadron move out, leaving 126 to play with its new aircraft and build up its personnel numbers. Conversion training continued until the last postings-in on 21 May signified its full complement and the squadron moved to Culmhead the following day. The 42 Group detachment duly removed the unused fuel stocks on 24 May.

MM273, 'P', one of the rarely-photographed Mosquito PR16 of 4 Squadron. It arrived at Sawbridgeworth only two weeks prior to the squadron leaving (for Gatwick) due to failure of the starboard engine during conversion training at Aston Down necessitating an engine change on site there.

Photo by the late Frank Andrews, via Philip Birtles

Surely the largest aircraft ever to land at Sawbridgeworth, the 88' 0" wingspan Airspeed Horsa Mk 2 of HGCU which force-landed in October 1944 and stayed for a month.

1994 aerial view looking north-east over the airfield site with the Much Hadham Road crossing the centre of the picture. Shingle Hall is on the right with Blounts Farm on the left and Mathams Wood behind it. The remaining perimeter track is much in evidence but traces of the sections removed can be seen near Shingle Hall.

The author's children display samples of airfield lighting recovered from the site. The 12" x 8" flarepath fitting carries two pygmy bulbs whilst the 8" diameter C5 'crossbar' fitting only has one.

Without realising it 126 Squadron had been the last flying unit at Sawbridgeworth and left, to all intents and purposes, an operational station able to receive and deal with aircraft, this capability being aptly demonstrated on three further occasions prior to the war's end.

The station was now without any resident squadrons, only the odd communications aircraft being present until they too were transferred elsewhere, and on 1 June W/C Bristow was posted away and replaced by S/L Gordon Sudworth. Sudworth had the unenviable task of overseeing the run-down of what had been a fairly active station, now reduced to a transit camp for mobile units en route to France and Belgium who only stayed for a matter of weeks at a time.

Robots and Rockets

RAF Sawbridgeworth played no part in Operation 'Overlord', the largest military operation of all time, but three weeks afterwards began to experience a new kind of warfare when the first of the German revenge weapons, the V1, appeared in the skies over southern England.

Whether it was called the 'buzz-bomb', 'doodle-bug', 'diver' or 'fly' the effect the Luftwaffe's FZG76 flying bomb had on those under its flightpath was the same. When the sound of the Argus pulse-jet engine was heard coming the general prayer was "keep going, keep going". If it passed over you were lucky, someone else was going to get it, but if it stopped there was an agonising silence of some 10–15 seconds before the tumbling weapon came to earth and the 1850lb warhead exploded on impact. Between the end of June and the middle of August five flying bombs fell in the vicinity, the closest being at Exnells Farm just to the west of the airfield, but luckily no casualties resulted. Eventually double agents on the Continent fed false reports to German contacts on impact locations such that areas to the north of London ceased to be affected by 'overshots'. The agents' brief was to convince the Luftwaffe that the majority of the missiles were already passing London, their principal target, and falling in open farmland. This was of course true for a small number of the missiles fired but was enough to have the launch crews lower the range so that London received 'overshots' whereas Kent and Sussex then took the brunt of the attack.

By August 1944 the Allies had over-run all the coastal launch sites and the V1 offensive stopped, but the following month a greater menace arrived, the V2 long-range rocket.

Whilst the V1 was basically an aircraft just smaller than a fighter that could be intercepted or brought down by AA fire or the balloon barrage, the Army-launched V2 was different, and there was no defence against it. The fixed launch sites for the V1 were attacked and destroyed by 170 Squadron amongst others but the V2, a 14-ton rocket carrying a one-ton warhead, was fired from mobile launchers to arrive out of the upper air without any warning and cause destruction on an unprecedented scale, much greater even than the RAF's 'Tallboy' weapons dropped by 9 and 617 Squadrons. Due to its ultimate re-entry speed in the region of 3,600 mph it exploded before its supersonic shock waves reached the ground.

Two rockets landed near the airfield in January 1945, the site being lucky to escape the V-weapon onslaught, whereas Stapleford Tawney to the south had a V2 fall in the very centre of the airfield in November 1944. The area around Sawbridgeworth received its share of both V1 and V2 but whilst property was damaged only one casualty resulted. In that same seven-month period no enemy bombing attacks were reported, the only incident of note being a 4,000 lb RAF bomb dropped in error near to Hadham Park Farm which damaged property at Bury Green

Cuckoos

The B26 Marauder, with its notorious lack of single-engined performance, was well known to 9th Air Force crews, in particular those operating from nearby Stansted (USAF Station 169) who were thankful for the landing facilities still afforded by Sawbridgeworth. The main runway at Stansted practically aligned with runway 24 at Sawbridgeworth and it was a simple matter, if an engine failed on take-off, to set up a landing on the field. One such event occurred on 12 August 1944 after 42107611 (K9–F) 'Chicago Cyclone' of the 344th BG lost an engine on its second mission of the day. Bombs were jettisoned and, with hydraulic systems inoperable, Lt John D Ashford made a belly landing on the grass surface finally ending up near Bursteads. The bomber suffered little damage and did not catch fire, the three injured crew members being treated by the emergency services and station sick quarters staff.

Exactly one month later on 12 September another B26 nearly landed at Sawbridgeworth after its prop gearing went but, on approaching the airfield, the pilot saw that tractors were out mowing the tracked and grass areas. He circled until the Stansted circuit was clear of departing aircraft and landed safely downwind there.

Sawbridgeworth received its penultimate 'cuckoo' on 21 September when, after dropping off a glider and Polish paratroops in support of the ill-fated Arnhem operation, a USAF C47 made a force-landing with engine problems. The aircraft, from 315th TCG, was soon repaired and left the next day.

The last airborne emergency came less than a month later on 16 October when a Horsa landed with its controls unserviceable. The glider, from the HGCU at Fairford, had been on tow behind a 190 Squadron Stirling en route for Great Dunmow prior to being taken out to Italy when the problem arose. It cast the tow whilst in range of the airfield and landed safely to await repairs, the crew of two being sent to Dunmow by road. The pace of life was much slower now with the war moving away as the Allies gained more ground on the Continent, subsequently repairs were not completed for nearly a month. Eventually, on 10 November, a Whitley arrived to tow the Horsa out, the combination leaving easily and safely. This was the last recorded aircraft movement and although the revitalised emergency services were held on standby to deal with any further arrivals other personnel were left to tidy up their affairs before being posted away.

The last days

One of the last events held on the airfield was a football match on 26 November 1944 between personnel from the station and 211 MU from Hyde Hall. No result was recorded as the match was terminated early due to the tragic death of one player, Cpl Cooper from 211 MU, critically injured during a normal tackle. His funeral, the last involving personnel from Sawbridgeworth, was at Bishops Stortford on 4 December.

The station was transferred to Maintenance Command on 30 November and the pace of life slowed right down. The airfield lighting was de-commissioned, white 'out of use' crosses were put at the approaches to all runways and many of the hutted areas on dispersed sites and nearby farms began to be cleared, leaving only the permanent structures standing.

This however, once again, was not quite the end of station life for on 12 April 1945 yet another unit established itself on site when 247 MU moved in to operate as a Packed Aviation Fuel and Aero Engine Lubricating store. Personnel establishment, according to Order LWE/MC/6351, was to be a Squadron Leader as CO, one WAAF, six officers and about 305 Airmen, all accommodated on the Communal and Officers' Quarters sites with officers in the Officers' Mess. Marching-in was completed on 17 April and, with accounting facilities provided by 211 MU at Hyde Hall, rations and medical aid were catered for by RAF Hunsdon.

The day after marching-in saw the first despatches of fuel going by road convoy to 8th Air Force stations at Rivenhall, Gt Dunmow, Blakehill Farm, Broadwell, Shepherds Grove and Andrewsfield. These continued until 23 April when the total of 100AV/150 fuel issued in jerry-cans was 104,500, or 350 tons. Replenishment stocks arrived from Stanlow and Beaulieu, again in jerry-cans.

The concept of a central depot for fuel despatch continued until it was found necessary to have a form of mobile sub-depot at various airfields as distribution points in order to speed up journey times. A mobile POL flight was therefore established at Ipswich between 9–11 May comprising one officer, a sergeant and 57 ORs with twelve 3-ton vehicles to see if the scheme was viable. The idea worked and, after a change in personnel, another detachment was at Ipswich from 19–23 May and 26–27 June before moving up to RAF Pulham.

Due to Hunsdon closing in May the provision of medical facilities was transferred to RAF Matching, and on 7 June the MU became self-catering with rations drawn direct from the RASC at Danesbury Park.

July saw a drop in deliveries due to a 'go slow' by London dockers, causing the airmen to be redeployed to duties on the airfield site including ground defence training courses.

On 20 August 211 MU at Great Hyde Hall closed down and 247 MU then became self-accounting, which was just as well as it coincided with a period of limited POL movements. Gradually airmen were released from service under the General Release Scheme, although these losses were offset by more being continually posted in, pending their own release. This put an extra strain on the Admin section which had not been up to establishment since the unit was formed. RAF Matching then closed in October and the MU had to cater for all its own requirements.

Commanding officers changed frequently whilst personnel numbers remained similar, and to offset boredom use was made of the sports facilities still remaining, with added features of a dance and an ENSA show both held in the gymnasium in November. Christmas 1945 passed and, on 31 January 1946, 263 MU at Stansted took over the provision of accounting facilities.

A fire in the POL office/SHQ on 26 February destroyed a number of items of working clothes before being extinguished, the 6 remaining WAAFs were posted away the next day but, most important of all, film shows and sports were still continuing.

March saw the Herts War Agricultural Committee start to plough up parts of the airfield for wheat sowing, the airfield lighting was removed from the runways and perimeter track, and the Allens Green road was then re-opened to the public as that part of the site was relinquished.

In April demobilisation lectures started to be given to all ranks, and the gymnasium cinema projection equipment was dismantled, indicating that closure of the unit was imminent. Disbandment was planned for 1 May but the next unit to arrive could not commence the marching-in until 2 May at least. The eventual handover was on 16 May 1946 when 3 MU took over the Communal Site and Officers' Quarters.

3 MU at Sawbridgeworth was one of five sub-sites to its HQ at Milton, Berkshire and dealt primarily with the disposal of surplus service material. In total 3 MU had under its wing some 2,100 personnel, plus 180 German PoWs and 30 Italian co-operators, spread around its various locations. Its monthly target for transfer of stock to Equipment Disposal depots was in the order of 2,000 tons, which it achieved consistently right through until 1948. The sub-site at Sawbridgeworth, with its complement of seven RAF officers, two WAAFs, 140 other ranks and 400 civilians, met its targets until its closure in June 1947, as well as participating in inter-Service competitions such as the annual fire-fighting efficiency which was won in 1946 by a team made up from all the 3 MU sub-sites. An emergency was dealt with in February 1947 when, in order to relieve the load on the National Grid, the Air Ministry Works Department brought back into use the 1942 Standby electrical equipment in Building 3 on the Communal Site to maintain the essential Unit services on the station.

Squatters

On 30 September 1946 with the military presence now diminishing but the farmers not in complete control of the previously-requisitioned land, nine families of squatters moved into buildings on the SSQ, W/T site and part of the airfield which fell in High Wych parish, namely the WAAF site. Sawbridgeworth District Council had no power to prevent this and over a short period of time more families established homes on sites 1, 2 and 3 simply by removing the Air Ministry padlocks to gain entry to the huts. As the Handcraft and Nissen huts became overcrowded families simply split them up by hanging blankets to form partitions.

Before the District Council could exercise any form of control it first had to improve living conditions by supplying Elsan toilets and a limited mains water supply. The Ministry of Health then insisted that Sawbridgeworth act as agent in management of the camp and Braughing District

Council agreed to bear the cost of installing mains water and electricity to the occupied buildings. The provision of new services went ahead, as well as the implementation of rent collections, whilst the MoH considered making further improvements to the dwellings defined by them as temporary accommodation. Rents had been set per week, depending on the area of hut occupied, but by 3 October two more families moved in and six more had taken possession by 6 February 1947 to upset the balance even more. This increased to 24 by June, a total of 87 persons being on various sites, and only the presence of 3 MU on the Communal Site prevented this also being taken over at this time. An RAF liaison officer had been consulted and saw no objection to the Council upgrading the accommodation to take 30 families in total but, after the WAAFs and civilian workers left in March and 3 MU itself closed down at the end of June, tenant numbers increased far beyond the 25% anticipated.

In July rents started to fall into arrears and the Council decided to write off the initial losses, but in August the Air Ministry then dropped a bombshell by issuing notices to the squatters stating that they would be collecting amounts to cover water and electricity supplied. As all the promised improvements had not been completed other rents began to be unpaid, but this was only part of the continuing saga of arrears. In November, with a total of 131 persons on site, the MoH were initiating the transfer of buildings and land on the WAAF and Communal Sites from the AM to the MoH for the Council's use for temporary housing purposes. The Ministry pointed out that it was not relinquishing its control of the land or the huts at this time but merely expecting the District Council, as the housing authority, to manage the camp until it was possible to rehouse the occupants.

At this time Sawbridgeworth War Memorial Committee had approached the Air Ministry to have the camp gymnasium released to them as a memorial hall, and requested that it be kept locked until the decision of the Regional Disposals Office was known. The decision was eventually made in their favour and, in 1948, plans put into motion to dismantle the entire structure and re-assemble it on a suitable site in the town centre. The operation took nearly two years to accomplish, the building being re-erected in The Forebury and subsequently enlarged, with the memorial wall tablet being laid by the Chairman of the Memorial Hall Fund on 31 December 1949 to commence its new lease of life as a lasting memorial to the people of Sawbridgeworth who gave their lives in two World Wars.

As the harsh winter of 1947/48 set in living conditions on the camp sites resembled those on the 1940 landing ground, but despite this many couples, young and old, made homes there. Daily routines became well-established, even down to the deliveries of milk and coal (for the few remaining RAF pot-bellied stoves, once the fuel supply of wooden doors and fittings stripped from other huts had run out). One incident of note concerned a young couple who, anxious to be living together legally, were married in the Register Office and found in the matrimonial bed that same afternoon by the coalman who called for his money.

In March 1948, in an attempt to solve the rent arrears problem, a review was made and rents fixed at between 5/- to 12/- (25–60p) per week, depending on the area of building occupied, for both the WAAF and Communal Sites. Some huts on the latter had to be demolished due to the state they were in, tenants having stripped them of all wooden items for winter fuel, but further water supply and sewage disposal measures were carried out. The cost of improvements to 22 huts on the High Wych Camp, as it became known, in June amounted to £666 with a further £764 being expended on electrical work.

At this time Captain Edward Morris of Bursteads was connected to the main power supply at the Communal Site and presented with a bill for £86, which he naturally contested. Up to this time Bursteads, like many other local farms, had no electricity even though the nearby military had been supplied during the war. The matter continued until December, when it was settled by a compensation award made to Captain Morris for the use of his land at Blounts as an airfield and Bursteads as billets during the war years (when he had to stay at Tharbies Lodge). The award was back-dated to 1940 and set at a maximum of £4/5/0 (£4.25) per year.

The occupation of the camp sites continued into 1949, there now being in existence a camp committee called the Parsonage Estate and District Welfare and Social Club. This authority acted for the tenants in liaising with the Council on housing matters mostly to do with improvements, which were generally given, even though the old problem of rent arrears was still current. However when the committee made approaches to Sawbridgeworth Council in July for two large buildings on the Communal Site (nos 3 and 4) to be adapted for housing they were told that this would not happen, as legal proceedings were in hand to recover part of the arrears to a value of £427, and that the WAAF site would be abandoned but some necessary work would be carried out on existing huts. Finally, in September 1949, Braughing District Council took a firm hand and commenced a rehousing programme whereby most families were put into newly-built council properties in the Bishops Stortford area, and the Communal and living sites passed back to the owners, the Church Commissioners, for agricultural purposes once more. The WAAF site was cleared completely and the fields on the east side of the airfield became so large that they took on the appearance of prairies, such were the trends coming into farming at that time.

Demolition work

With the airfield and dispersed sites now back to agriculture the farmers faced a huge dilemma. As most buildings had been desecrated by misuse, and the removal of fixtures and fittings, they took on the appearence of ghostly shells which left no alternative but to demolish the majority of them. This 'tidying' phase started in 1950 and continued for three years in between normal farm routines.

Whilst farming demands required some structures to be retained for storage purposes those in the way of the large-field system now in common use had to be removed. One area to be given urgent attention was the dispersal and hardstands adjacent to Blounts, these and the short length of perimeter track up to the Much Hadham Road being cleared using steam engines (ah, shades of 1926!) with the work being completed by 1952.

The watch office, fire engine shed, NFE store and floodlight tractor/trailer buildings at Shingle Hall went literally in a blaze of glory in 1953 when the farm enlisted the help of a local builder to bring down the concrete structures with explosives, before taking out the perimeter track they were situated on.

In May 1956, coincident with the Air Ministry relinquishing its safeguarding of the entire site, the sole T2 hangar was dismantled. As the sale price the Ministry was asking was more than the Morris family could reasonably afford contractors took it down and shipped it away, the length of perimeter track from its base and northwards as far as the Much Hadham Road also being taken out. The nearby Link Trainer and AM Bombing Teacher buildings (53 and 26) were also taken down that same year to give more space, whilst the majority of the Blisters around the site remained to provide useful storage space.

Harry Roberts

The last operation mounted on the airfield, although carried out in a military manner, was a civilian one and of great necessity.

On 12 August 1966 near Wormwood Scrubs prison in Shepherds Bush, West London, an attempted robbery was unwittingly foiled by police officers in an unmarked 'Q' car doing a routine vehicle check. During the confrontation the three officers were murdered in the call of duty, with the three perpetrators fleeing the scene of the crime. The three, John Duddy, John Witney and Harry Roberts went on the run and, although the first two were captured soon after, Roberts eluded the grasp of the police and disappeared.

Sightings of Roberts soon came in from all round the capital, as well as West Essex where he had been variously reported in Abridge, Theydon Bois and Epping. Once again he disappeared and it was known that he had previously bought camping gear which, coupled with the fact that he had done his National Service in Malaya, indicated that he was going to live rough in the countryside by utilising the skills of survival, camouflage and camping learnt from the Army.

HERTS & ESSEX

OBSERVER

INCORPORATING SAFFRON WALDEN AND DISTRICT OBSERVER

No. 6211 Established 1861 | Telephone Bishop's Stortford 2401, 2402, 2403 | FRIDAY, NOVEMBER 18, 1966 | Registered at the G.P.O. as a Newspaper | G | PRICE

96-DAY MANHUNT ENDS IN A BISHOP'S STORTFORD WOOD

Mrs. Joy Lewin, who sold groceries to Roberts.

'I saw Roberts' stories pour in

YES, we saw Harry Roberts. . . . This is the local reaction from hundreds of Bishop's Stortford residents, shopkeepers, publicans, and many others following the dramatic arrest of Roberts, after 96 days of freedom, in a hangar used for storing cattle fodder near Thorley on Tuesday.

Since the news of Roberts' arrest the Observer office has been flooded with reports from people who have seen him. From two boys who discovered his hide-out over a fortnight ago and told their mother they thought it was Roberts. From a local shopkeeper who served Roberts every Wednesday afternoon and who called him "the polite man." From workmen who saw him walking along the road and later missed oil from their road lamps, and from many others who allege they saw him in Bishop's Stortford shopping.

On Wednesday—the day after arrest by two Hertfordshire police sergeants—it was a day of [illegible] in the town.

It was also a day of relief [illegible] up by a local resident [illegible] after hearing the news. [illegible] I can now unlock [illegible] window."

It was also a day when many local people blamed themselves for not recognising Roberts. "If [illegible] connected this man with Roberts he might have been [illegible]," said one [illegible] in the Thorley area [illegible] saw Roberts on several [illegible].

HIGH DRAMA

Never before has Bishop's Stortford seen so much activity [illegible] high drama which can best [illegible] of events.

It was late on Monday evening that local police became convinced that Harry Roberts was occupant of a tent found in Thorley Wood [illegible].

Detective Superintendent [illegible] Chitty, who has been [illegible] the huge manhunt for [illegible] since the shooting of three London policemen in [illegible] arrived at Bishop's Stortford to look over articles found in the tent.

A guard was placed on the [illegible] which was [illegible] in Thorley [illegible] along with some camping equipment until the following [illegible] when a search was [illegible].

On Tuesday morning policemen from many parts of Hertfordshire began arriving in Bishop's Stortford [illegible] the hunt [illegible].

After a short briefing in the police station canteen in the [illegible] set off on an inch by inch search of the [illegible] area.

They had only been gone a short time when Roberts was unearthed.

Police Sergeant Peter Smith, from Stevenage, who is aged 33 and married with four children, entered an old hangar full of straw and stumbled upon a bottle of methylated spirit.

Lifting a straw bale he discovered Roberts lying in a sleeping bag. There was no struggle. He was then joined by Police Sergeant Oswald Thorne, from Hemel Hempstead, who with the help of local farmer Mr. W. Morris, of [illegible] steads, Spellbrook Lane, took Roberts in Mr. Morris' blue Land Rover to Stortford Police Station.

Colin Mills with Bambi.

Here, dramatically, at 11.45 a.m. police issued a statement confirming that the man was in fact Roberts.

As this news spread the road outside Bishop's Stortford police station became crowded with onlookers. Even the cemetery of St. Michael's Church opposite was crowded with people and Press photographers.

The biggest manhunt ever staged in Britain was over.

Then Roberts came out. He was driven from the station in a black police van escorted by two police cars and a motor cyclist. The crowd jeered and the drama was now complete.

The two police sergeants who arrested Roberts — Sergt. Peter Smith (left) and Sergt. Oswald Thorne.

The Land Rover that brought Harry Roberts to the side door of Bishop's Stortford police station.

Boys saw tent two weeks ago

Three Bishop's Stortford boys came across Roberts' tent nearly two weeks ago. At the time they joked about it being Roberts and told their parents—who didn't give it a second thought.

Housewife Mrs. Marjorie Mills, mother of two of the boys, Terence (16) and Colin, said at her 7, Thornbera Road home the day after Roberts was arrested: "They said they found a tent in Thorley Wood and that someone was living there. They laughed about Harry Roberts being there."

She went on: "They lifted up the side of the tent to look in, but whoever was in there switched on a radio and they left. They saw there was a man inside the tent but that was all."

When they heard it was Roberts they only wished I had taken notice of what they said.

THRILLED

Colin, a 13-year-old pupil of Bishop's Stortford Boys' Secondary School, was taken from his class by police on Tuesday morning to identify a tent at Thorley Wood. "He was thrilled about seeing the car he was in on television," said Mrs. Mills.

Colin told an Observer reporter of how he went for a walk with his brother and friend Raymond Lawrence, of 9, Norfolk Way, Bishop's Stortford. They took the Mills' Whippet, Bambi, for its exercise.

"We saw the tent and I thought it was Scouts camping there, then Terry joked about Harry Roberts. But I didn't pay much attention to it," he said.

He recalled: "My schoolfriends didn't believe at all that I had seen the tent—until the police came and took me in a big white car to Thorley Wood to identify it."

Colin, who has no ambition to become a policeman, said his brother found the tent open and empty when he saw it again on Saturday.

CAMOUFLAGED

Terry later told the reporter that he was the first to spot the tent. It was so well camouflaged that they nearly walked into it.

"As soon as I mentioned Roberts' the person inside the tent switched on a radio," he added.

Mr. W. Morris, the farmer who owns Mathams Wood, saw Roberts arrested then drove him in a blue Land Rover with a police escort into Stortford.

While Roberts was inside Bishop's Stortford police station large crowds waited outside. Pictured above is a section of the crowd of sightseers, Press, and television men in Basbow Lane.

When this picture was taken early on Tuesday Sergt. Oswald Thorne (left), seen in conference with a colleague, did not know that three hours later he would be one of the men who arrested Roberts.

REWARD CLAIMED

MR. John Cunningham (21), a gypsy living in a caravan at Thorley Lane, Bishop's Stortford, has claimed the £1,000 reward offered by Scotland Yard for information leading to the capture of Harry Roberts.

On Wednesday, Mr. Cunningham visited Bishop's Stortford police station to make his claim and was told to get in touch by letter with the Metropolitan Police Commissioner.

Polite man who bought groceries

Every Wednesday afternoon for the past six weeks a "polite man" bought provisions at the Farm Stores, a grocery shop in Thorley Lane. The man was Harry Roberts.

After the first visit the shop's owner, 32-year-old Mrs. Joy Lewin, of Hayley Bell Gardens, said to her assistant and a customer: "Gosh! I think that's Harry Roberts." They laughed.

"So many people were ringing the police with false alarms that I decided to do nothing," added Mrs. Lewin. "I didn't want to look a fool.

"I could kick myself now," she said regretfully. "If I had told the police I would have saved everyone a lot of trouble."

The second time that Roberts came to the shop, Mrs. Lewin was on her own. "I was pretty nervous," she admitted, "but he was so natural and polite that I didn't mind. I think it was his eyes that made me so sure who it was."

Roberts used to buy a week's provisions of tinned food, butter, and powdered milk. He wore a [illegible] jacket, dark trousers, and boots and paid for his goods in half-crowns.

"I thought he might be a gypsy or a roadworker." But when police called at the shop [illegible] with a photograph [illegible]

After many false sightings police deductions led them to believe that he had crossed into Hertfordshire and a Headquarters was set up in Bishops Stortford. In fact Roberts had been quite active in the county for some time, buying food in Thorley and even taking his mid-day meals in cafes near to the police station in Bishops Stortford, but it was the frequent reports of an unkempt, bearded stranger seen in Thorley woods, south of the town, that made police concentrate their searches there. Following statements by children that a tented camp had been found in the woods police began sweeping that area. Apart from the obvious traces of someone having been living there, and instances of break-ins to local factories such as Walter Lawrences in Sawbridgeworth for money and confectionery, no trace of him came to light. Finally, after a reward was posted, an informant gave police the news that he was somewhere on the old airfield, and that area was cordoned off whilst police search units moved in.

After searching buildings on the outlying and dispersed sites police moved to the blister hangars near Shingle Hall where, at around noon on 15 November 1966, Roberts was found bivouacked behind hay bales in EO blister no 5. He gave up without a struggle and after 96 days on the run, of which at least 42 were spent in the Sawbridgeworth area, was moved in farmer William Morris' Land-Rover under guard to Bishops Stortford police station. After being charged he was transferred to London where he, along with the other two accused, was brought before Mr Justice Glyn-Jones at the Central Criminal Court on 6 December. Roberts received the sentence of at least 30 years 'at Her Majesty's Pleasure'. Thus ended the last action at Sawbridgeworth where at Blounts, three quarters of a mile from where he was found, police had set up a field HQ and the Civil Defence manned a canteen in support of the operation to find him. The press had a field day, although the TV news items were slightly wrong in screening pictures of the blister hangar at Blounts Farm, instead of the one Roberts used and was caught in.

Crop spraying

To cope with the large size of farm fields being worked in 1959 the Morris family, in keeping with current trends, employed aerial crop-sprayers to lay top-dressing and do slugbait spraying in order to speed up the growing processes. Fisons Farmwork from Feering, near Colchester, was then using DH Tiger Moths as well as the Chipmunk Mk 23 that was coming into fashion for this sort of work. Both types were fitted with under-fuselage hoppers and wing spray-bars, although the Tigers were later fitted with atomisers fixed one per wing to the interplane struts, and when spraying landed on the remaining portion of perimeter track close to Shingle Hall or in firm pasture for refuelling and refilling with chemicals. When Fisons ceased operations in 1969 the company changed to Fieldspray Ltd and continued the contracts, using its own fixed-wing aircraft as well as leasing helicopters of the Hiller 360 type which were landed in fields close to the work for R & R to cut down the ground time between sorties. While at Sawbridgeworth Fieldspray always referred to it as 'Bill Morris's airfield', and used it as a central base for other contracts as well as work at Shingle Hall or Blounts Farms.

When the contract with Fieldspray ended the work was taken on in 1978 by Bowker Air Services, based at Rush Green near Hitchin. Aircraft types had also changed, Bowkers having progressed from its days as Farm Aviation with Tiger Moths to using the specially-designed Piper Pawnee and Grumman AgCat for the work. Ministry directives then brought an end to pesticide spraying in 1983 and the crop-sprayers were limited to carrying out top-dressing however, with even the older aircraft types in use, the cost of aerial spraying eventually became too prohibitive and was discontinued in 1988. The mobile boom sprayers mounted on tractors and produced by Scherings, successors to Crop Culture who had carried out camouflaging of airfield sites in WW2, then took over and are still in use now.

The plane at the pub

The last 'military' aircraft movement at Sawbridgeworth came about in 1970 and terminated at a most unlikely place, the forecourt of the Queen's Head public house in Allens Green, wartime haunt for groundcrews. The publican, George Jackson, had been with 11 Squadron flying Hawker

Hurricanes in the Western Desert and on hearing that one of the Hurricane replicas from the 1968 film *The Battle of Britain* was lying in a cold storage yard near Bishops Stortford promptly bought it. The static external replica (SER), later to be given the British Aviation Preservation Council number BAPC 73, had been built substantially of wood at Pinewood Studios in 1968 and looked very realistic.

For the benefit of the pub's business the SER was moved there, put in position next to the car park as an outside attraction and, with spotlights later added, stayed until the publican decided to move on. With its wings removed it was towed away in January 1975 on its own wheels en route to a new home in Haverhill, Suffolk, but a wheel bearing failed on the A11 and it sat in a lay-by at Ugley for one week whilst repairs were made. Its subsequent whereabouts are unknown, but what is certain is that of all the aircraft types at Sawbridgeworth it was only the second Hurricane to serve there.

Ghosts

Most airfields, army camps, castles or churches in England are credited with reports of supernatural sightings, and Sawbridgeworth is no exception. The sightings here first came to light in 1988 when Stephen Day was using Warren/Exnells/Cates Green Lane (known by these local names, the County Council only refer to it as unclassified road 3U42), west of the airfield, on his way to work from the Much Hadham Road.

He saw an apparition, in the form of an American airman kitted out for flying, on the roadside verge near the front gate to Warren Farm and thought it strange for someone to be dressed like that nowadays. On a later occasion both Stephen and his wife saw the figure, which also wore a flying helmet and carried a parachute pack in one hand. Since the initial sighting it has been seen in full from head to toe on many occasions, whether by day or night, each at a different time but always on the same spot. The sightings have continued into the 1990's and been so frequent that Stephen is not bothered by the presence, but expects to see it every time he passes and is somewhat disappointed when it is not there.

Whilst one of the 2 (AC) Squadron Mustang pilots, F/O W Shepherd, force-landed on take-off close to the VHF/DF hut which remains a short distance away, at a period in time when it could be said that the pattern of flying helmet then worn by AC pilots resembled that of the Americans, this was not a fatal incident (in fact Shepherd was found by his rescuers drinking tea in the nearby shepherds' house). Whereas four Mustang fatalities occurred on or near the airfield (three from 2 (AC) and one from 170 Squadrons) the only American fatality on the airfield during its active life that could be associated with the figure occurred on 3 April 1943 and involved a 2nd Lt Smolenski, pilot of a P47c Thunderbolt. The aircraft suffered an engine failure when in the vicinity and crashed in a field nearer to Green Tye as the pilot attempted a deadstick landing. Smolenski, from the 335 FS, 4 FG based at Debden, died in the crash fire before the fire services could reach him and, whilst the apparition does not appear to be burnt, it could be that it is his ghost that waits by the roadside for a lift back to base or that great airfield in the sky.

No sightings were reported prior to 1988 so why did it take 45 years to manifest itself, and on this spot?

What remains now

The few personnel attached to the First World War landing ground used temporary tented accommodation as required and as such no trace remains today to mark their existence, similarly the wide open spaces on Racecourse Field in West Road also do not betray the presence of Army units, but many of the properties in the town used by the Air Ministry in the Second World War either socially or for billets still remain and are in private ownership once again. These include Townsend House and Glenroy (now renamed), along with the United Services Club and several of the public houses. The house at Great Hyde Hall, once the HQ of squadrons and MUs, became Chantry Mount School postwar before assuming its current role of self-contained flats set in the still-splendid

Action shot of a Bowker Air Services Piper Pawnee at work over Morris' Farm, showing the massive under-fuselage hopper discharging its load of fertiliser.
Bill Bowker photo

The ex *Battle of Britain* film Hurricane replica in pasture behind the car park at the Queen's Head public house, Allens Green in the early 1970s.   *Photo: George Jackson via Rob Trundle*

One of the eleven blister hangars, in two sizes, erected around the airfield site. This last survivor at Blounts Farm was blown down in the October 1987 gales.   *Photo: Paul Francis, 1984*

grounds. The gatehouse guard rooms are now lodge cottages and only an isolated building, believed to be a Link Trainer hut but of an unusual pattern, remains at the side of the estate road that winds up to the house, past where Nissen huts previously occupied the grounds.

On the environs of the airfield itself the Station Sick Quarters site is the most complete, with its buildings intact and serving as the Clarklands Industrial Estate. One omission is the mortuary slab, taken out of Building 5 to allow extra working space. The adjacent W/T and domestic sites are now fields once more, except that the entrances to all these can be made out as gaps in the road verges along Parsonage Lane.

By comparison the Communal Site has only two buildings remaining, these being the large standby set house and the grocery store (Buildings 3 and 4). The former is now home to a removals company whilst the latter houses a firm producing fibre-glass boats and associated products. It is planned to build a bypass for Sawbridgeworth town to pass over this area, which will no doubt sweep past these buildings. The road leading past the site onto what had been the common field 'Underlands' before becoming the WAAF site, and known as 'Campfield' when occupied by squatters, now peters out into farmland after only a few yards.

Blounts Farm itself has changed little, but gone are the huts from the grounds. The base to the last EO Blister hangar (82/8) blown down in the 1987 gales, is now a tennis court whilst the site of the nearby 24,000 gallon bulk fuel installation (Building 28) is marked by a large fenced-off pile of earth. The Morris family now occupy all the areas of the house previously used as HQs for the squadrons or Photographic Sections, and the 'theatre' barn serves as stables. Some defence works still remain near Fiddlers Brook and at each end of the Allens Green road, and from the air the outline of the compass swinging base (72) and removed perimeter track can just be made out, but apart from the visible perimeter track winding across Blackacre Field towards Shingle Hall very little exists here to reveal the existence of a once-busy airfield site.

At Shingle Hall light industry, appropriately in the form of vehicle repair shops, has taken over the main workshops (Building 16) whilst the farm retains the armoury (11) and main stores (12) for storage and preparation of animal foods. The cattle sheds here are covered with the roof sheeting recovered from the last Blounts Farm blister, the southerly EO blister (82/7) having been lost due to arson (as was 82/1), whilst the parachute store (Building 14) has been modified to house the farm repair workshop. The guard room and fire tender shed (Buildings 34 and 35) are currently being used by an export company as offices and stores.

From Shingle Hall cross the Much Hadham Road and you are then back on the perimeter track which winds around the northern part of the airfield site. Follow it, past the site of 'A' Flight dispersal where Harry Roberts was found in EO Blister hangar 82/5, past the field wherein the barbed defence wire and runway tracking was piled postwar and up to Mathams Wood where the Battle HQ (59) and a pill-box still lurk.

Just before you reach the wood look in the field corner to your right, here remains a concrete emplacement for an early type of spigot mortar which in its anti-tank role would have been used as primary defence of the airfield by units of the Home Guard. Dumped in the nearby moat were many of the airfield runway lights removed postwar to make ploughing easier. Carry on around the wood, past the last aircraft pen (61/9), through the gap at Newsett to the area where the Advanced Landing Ground was, and before you again reach the road you are in the once-muddy fields where so much history has been made, where the Lysanders were . . .

Glossary of terms

AC	Army Co-operation
ACG	Airfield Construction Group
AILO	Air Intelligence Liaison Officer
AOP	Air Observation Post
Arty/R	close liaison flights with Army to assess accuracy of gunfire
BEF	British Expeditionary Force
BG	Bomb Group (American)
Bodyline	bomb damage assessment flights by high-level element of 35 Wing
C & M	Care and Maintenance
CO/OC	Officer in charge
cuckoo	aircraft having to land at an airfield other than its own
Drem Mk 2	type of airfield lighting system
EO Blister	(Extended Over) a 91' 0" wide curved-roofed hangar with no walls
1 foot/inch/yard	Imperial dimensions for 305/25.4/914mm
Handcraft hut	asbestos-clad building seven-segmented in cross-section
HGCU	Heavy Glider Conversion Unit
Jane hut	timber hut of corrugated iron outer and wire-reinforced felt inner skin
Lagoon	shipping recces off the Dutch coast
Link Trainer	ground simulator for providing flying training
MU	Maintenance Unit
mosaic	overlapping set of vertical air photos
NAAFI	Navy, Army & Air Force Institution
Nissen hut	semi-circular corrugated steel building in 16, 24 and 30 foot widths
Noball	PR of flying bomb sites
NCO	non-commissioned officer
NFE	night-flying equipment
oblique	air photo taken on a downward incline
OR	other ranks
ORB	Operations Record Book of unit, station or Command
Over Blister	an 85' 0" wide curved-roofed hangar with no walls
Overlord	code name for 1944 Allied invasion of Occupied Europe
POL	petrol, oil and lubricants
Pilots Notes	'drivers handbook' for aircraft type in use
Popular	PR sorties of the Dutch and Belgian coastline
PR(U)	photo reconnaissance (unit)
PoW	prisoner of war
RDF	Radio Direction Finding and Ranging equipment (Radar)
Ranger	mass intruder patrol against targets of opportunity
R & SU	Repair and Salvage Unit
Rhubarb	low-level fighter sortie to Europe under cover of cloud or bad weather
RASC	Royal Army Service Corps
SAA	small arms ammunition
SOE	Special Operations Executive
SHQ	Station Headquarters
SSQ	Station Sick Quarters
TAF	Tactical Air Force (for Overlord)
TAC/R	tactical reconnaissance
TT	target-towing
T2	transportable shed mk 2 (a large pitched-roof hangar)
T3	trainer version of the DH Mosquito
TCG	Troop Carrier Group (American)
V1,V2	German Vergeltungswaffe (Revenge Weapons)
VHF/DF	Very High Frequency/Direction Finding
watch office	RAF term for airfield flying control building
W/T	wireless telegraphy
WAAF	Women's Auxiliary Air Force

BUILDING REFERENCES
AIRFIELD SITE

No.	SAW	A.M. No.	Con	Description
1	391	3659/42	S	Aircraft Shed T2
4	65	9026/41	B	Latrines and Ablutions
5	–	–	–	Recording Barometer
6	26	3382/41	B	Balloon Filling Hut
7	167	12779/41	B	Watch Office
8	223	9098/41	B	Fire Tender Shelter
9	223	9098/41	B	N.F.E. store
10	223	9098/41	B	Floodlight Trailer and Tractor Shed
11	269	2201/42	B	Armoury
12	222	9096/41	B	Main Stores
13	223	9098/41	B	Lubricant and Inflammables Store – Type 'A'
14	69	11137/41	B	Parachute Store
15	33	12409/41	B	Gas Clothing and Respirator Store for 960
16	221	9094/41	B	Main Workshops
17	119	13241/41	B	Sub-Station
18	65	9026/41	B	Technical Latrines, 5 Lats. 3 Abluts.
19	–	–	–	Station Offices (at Shingle Hall)
19A	–	–	N	Payment and accounts Offices
19B	–	–	N	Payment and Accounts Offices
20	–	–		M & E Plinths Nos 1–5
21	65	9026/41	B	Technical Latrines, 5 Lats. 3 Abluts.
22	65	9026/41	B	Technical Latrines, 5 Lats. 3 Abluts.
23	65	9026/41	B	Technical Latrines, 5 Lats. 3 Abluts.
24	65	9026/41	B	Office Staff Latrines, 4 Lats, 6 Abluts.
25	341	14310/41	B&N	Crew and Briefing Block
26	363	6301/42		A.M. Bombing Teacher
	364	4772/42		
27	–	–	N	Salvage Store 72" x 16"
28	132	13083/41		Bulk petrol Installation – Aviation – 24,000 gallons
29	132	13083/41		Bulk Petrol Installation – Aviation – 24,000 gallons
30	130	4619/40		Bulk Petrol Installation – M.T. – 3,000 gallons
31	–	–	W	Pilots' Room
32	–	–		Photographic Block (at Blounts Farm)
33a	–	–	N	Defence Huts
33b	–	–	N	Defence Huts
34	223	9098/41	B	Guard and Fire Party House
34a	–	–	B	Picket Post
35	223	9098/41	B	Fire Tender House
36	303	1949/42	B	M.T. Offices
37	303	1949/42	B	M.T. Shed and Yard
38	124	10786/41	B	Speech Broadcasting Installation Building
38a	401	AC201/42	B	Cable Diversions Box
39	238	16461/41	B	Cannon Test Butt
40	60	147/41)	B	M.G. Range – 3 No Points
	299	2964/42)		
41	–	–	BB	W.D. Contractors Offices and Yard
42	–	–	BB	Old Canteen
42a	–	–	BB	Wash-up Building
42b	–	–	N	Ablutions and Latrines
42c	–	–	N	Barrack Hut
43	–	–		Squadron Offices (in Blounts Farmhouse)

No.	SAW	A.M. No.	Con	Description
44	371	2547/42	B	Squadron Offices (N)
44a	65	9026/41	B	Latrines and Ablutions, 4 Lats. 7 Abluts. 2 Ur.
45a	296	ACC33/41	B	Flight Offices
45b	296	ACC33/41	B	Flight Offices
45c	296	ACC33/41	B	Flight Offices
45d	296	ACC33/41	B	Flight Offices
45e	296	ACC33/41	B	Flight Offices
46	269	2201/42	B	Squadron Maintenance Block
47				Petrol Tank – 4,000 gallons (UG) (Tank Removed)
48	296	ACC33/41	B	Ablutions, Latrines and Drying Rooms: 4 Buckets, 4 Abluts.
49		–	N	Barrack Huts – Nos 1, 3–20
50	296	ACC33/41	B	Ablutions, Latrines and Drying Rooms: 4 Buckets, 4 Abluts.
51	–	–	PH	Gas Defence Centre
52a	68	11049/41	B	Sleeping Shelter
52b	68	11049/41	B	Sleeping Shelter
52c	68	11049/41	B	Sleeping Shelter
52d	68	11049/41	B	Sleeping Shelter
52e	68	11049/41	B	Sleeping Shelter
53	56	10640/41	B	Link Trainer Building
54	295	13469/41	S	High-level Water Tank – 60,000 gallons
55a	409	–	B	Ablutions and Latrines, 6 Lats, 7 Abluts.
55b	409	–	B	Ablutions and Latrines, 6 Lats. 7 Abluts.
56				Lecture Room (in barn at Shingle Hall)
57	288	1950/42	TBC	Signals Block
58	–	–	W	Hut, 30' x 15'
59	67	11008/41	B	Battle Headquarters
60	–	–	S	Observation Tower
61	63	7181/41	E	Aircraft Pens – Blenheim Type – Nos 1–13
62	–	–	BB	S.A.A. Stores
63	–	–		Defence Headquarters (in Blounts Cottages)
64	–	–	B	Signals Office
65	–	–	CI	Ablutions
66	–	–	BB	Dining Room and Institute
69	–	–	B	S.C.I. workshop
70	–	–	BB	S.C.I. Store
71	131	11270/40		Bulk Oil Installation – 3,500 gallons
72	54	10836/40	C	Compass Platform
73	298	FCW4881	C	T.E. Hardstandings – Nos 1–3
74	298	FCW4881	C	S.E. Hardstandings – Nos 1–12
81	–	12512/41	–	O. Blister Hangars – Nos 1–3
82	–	12532/41	–	E.O. Blister Hangars – Nos 1–8
88	–	–	½N	Anti-gas Clothing and Equipment Stores
95	–	–	N	Hut
96	–	–	–	Salvage Compound (temp)

Construction of buildings

Breeze Blocks	shown	BB	Air Raid Shelter	shown	S [⌐⌐]
Brick	shown	B	Blast Shelter	shown	┼
Brick and Nissen	shown	BN	Pill Box	shown	● PB
Corrugated Iron	shown	CI			
Handcraft Hut	shown	H	**On plans solid shading or hatched areas**		
Janes Hut	shown	J	**indicate buildings still extant in 1995**		
Nissen	shown	N			
Plasterboard Hut	shown	PH	**On the airfield site layouts: Scale = 1:3000**		
Steel	shown	S	(approximately 21" = 1 mile)		

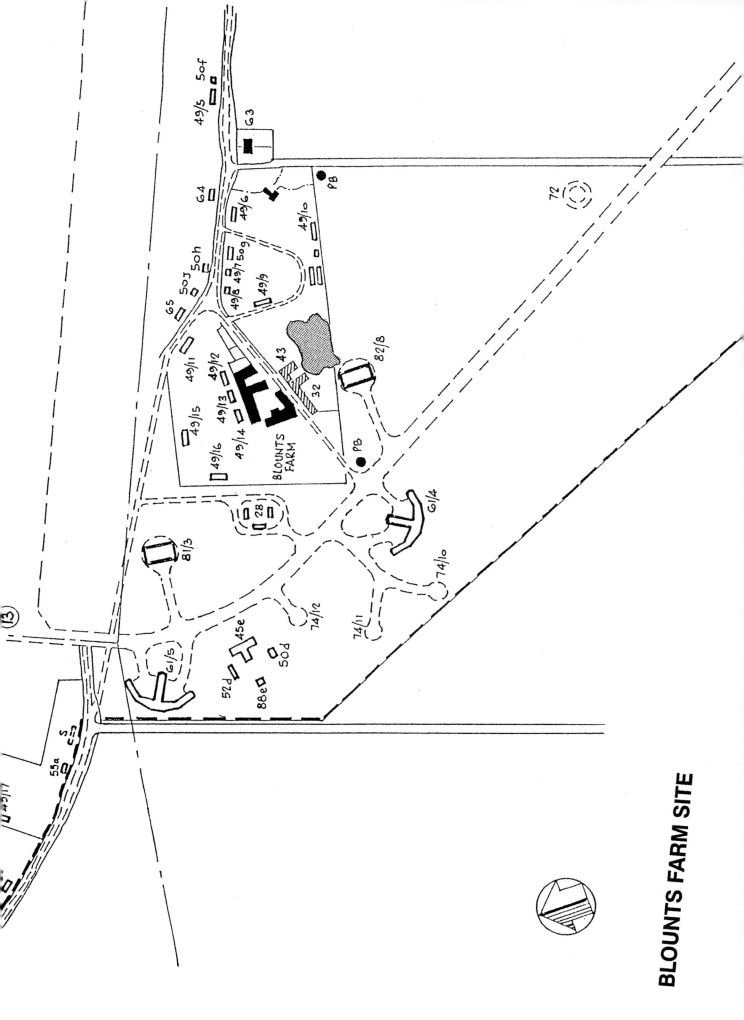

BLOUNTS FARM SITE

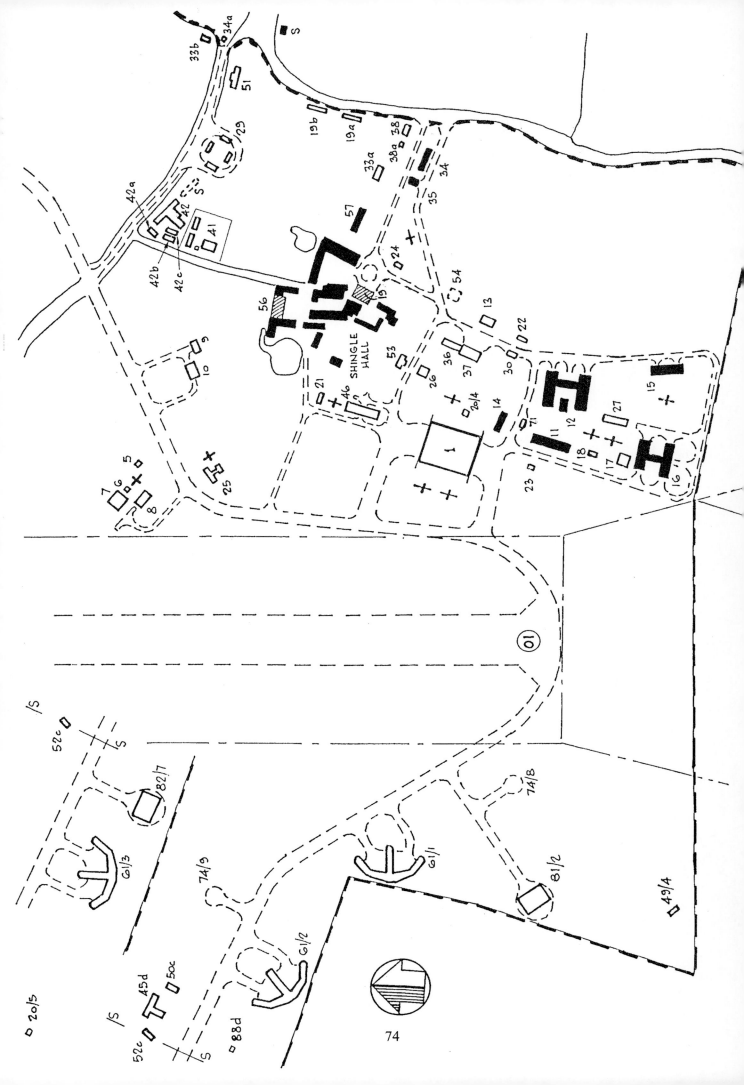

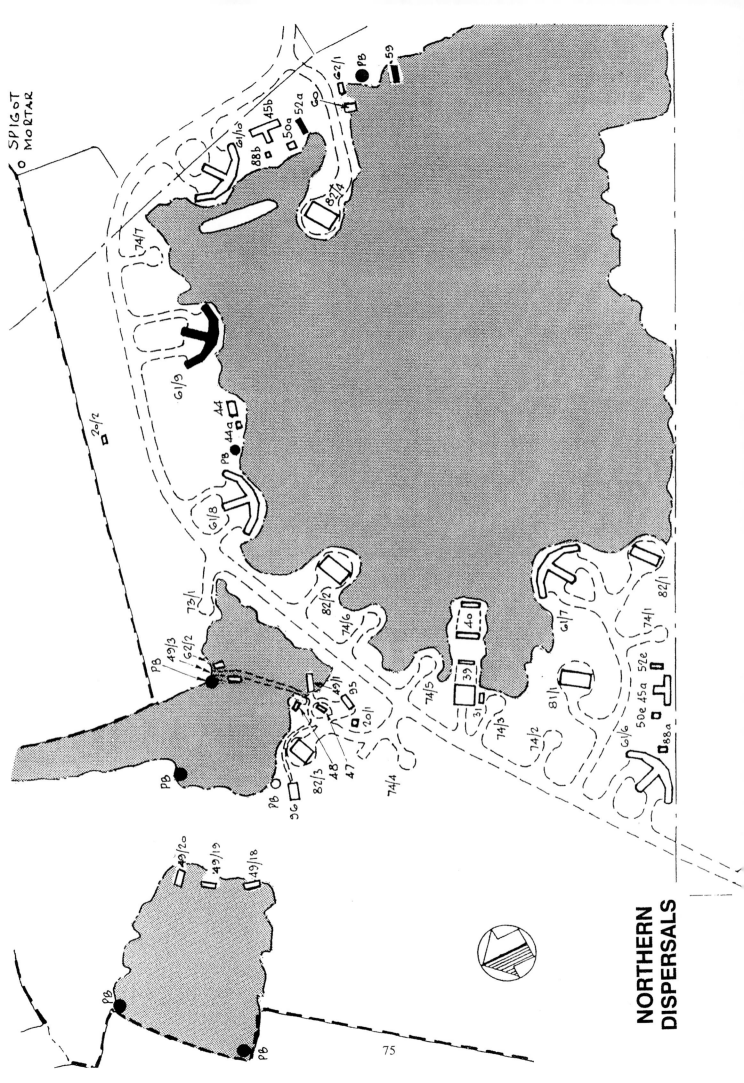

SPIGOT
MORTAR

O

62/1
PB
59

61/a
88b
45b
50a
52a
60

74/1

2/2

61/9

44
44a
PB

61/8

87/4

73/1
82/2
74/6

49/3
62/2
PB

49/1
95

20/1

82/3
48
47

74/4

36
PB

PB

PB

40
39
31

74/5

74/3

74/2

81/1

61/7

50e 45a 52e
88a
61/6

82/1

74/1

49/20
49/19
49/18

PB

PB

PB

NORTHERN
DISPERSALS

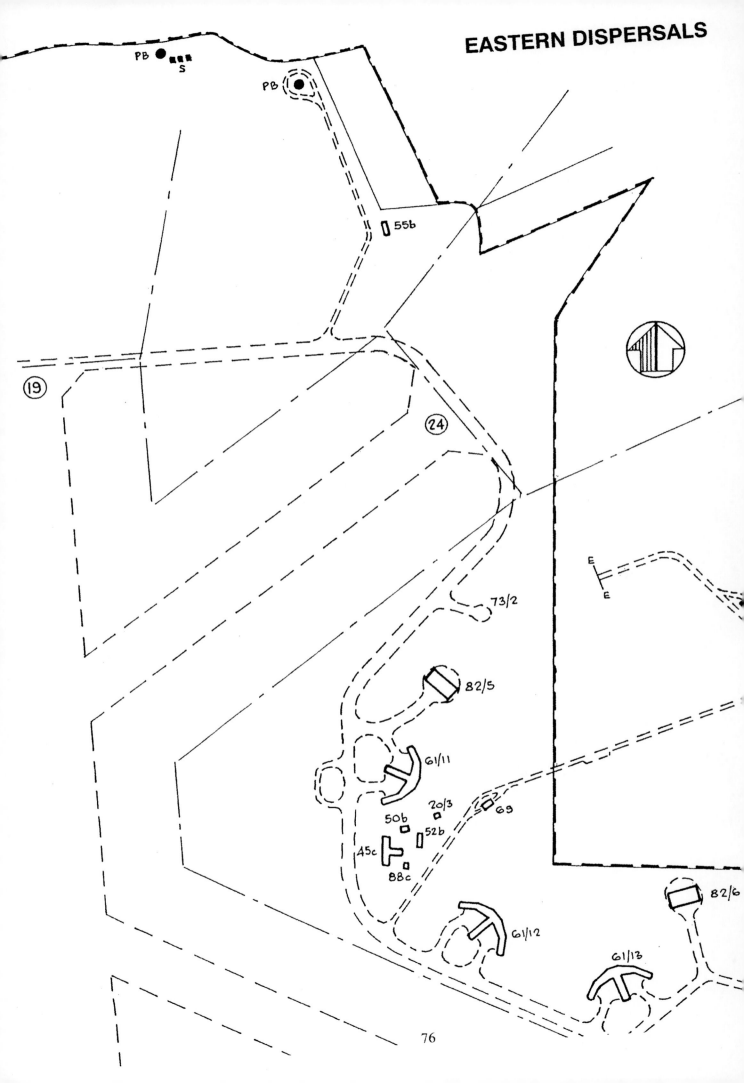

EASTERN DISPERSALS

PB

S

PB

55b

19

24

73/2

82/5

61/11

20/3

69

50b

52b

45c

88c

82/6

61/12

61/13

E
E

76

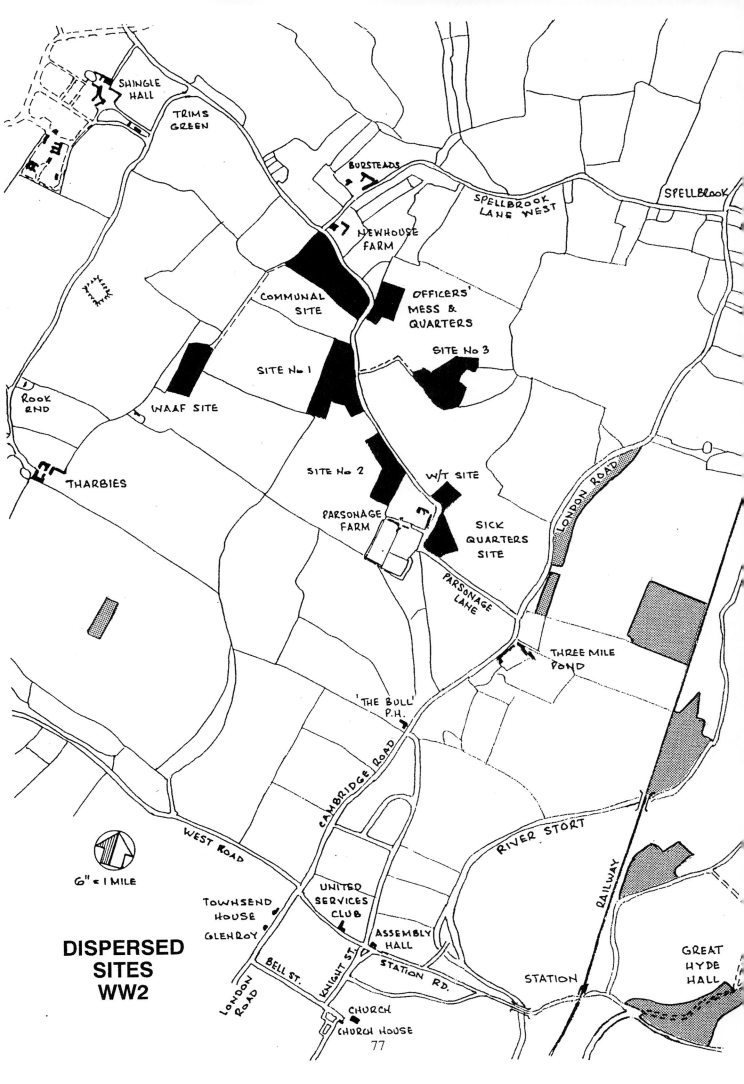

SHINGLE HALL

TRIMS GREEN

BURSTEADS

SPELLBROOK LANE WEST

SPELLBROOK

NEWHOUSE FARM

COMMUNAL SITE

OFFICERS' MESS & QUARTERS

SITE No 3

SITE No 1

WAAF SITE

ROOK END

SITE No 2

W/T SITE

THARBIES

PARSONAGE FARM

SICK QUARTERS SITE

LONDON ROAD

PARSONAGE LANE

THREE MILE POND

'THE BULL' P.H.

CAMBRIDGE ROAD

6" = 1 MILE

WEST ROAD

RIVER STORT

RAILWAY

TOWNSEND HOUSE

GLENROY

UNITED SERVICES CLUB

ASSEMBLY HALL

GREAT HYDE HALL

DISPERSED SITES WW2

BELL ST.

KNIGHT ST.

STATION R.D.

STATION

LONDON ROAD

CHURCH

CHURCH HOUSE

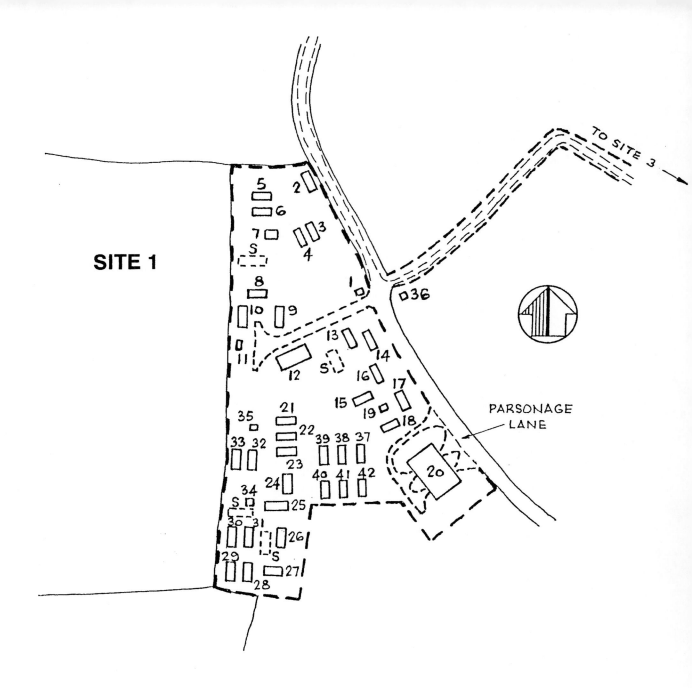

SITE 1

PARSONAGE LANE

On the dispersed site layouts – Scale = 1:2000 (approximately 32" = 1 mile)

Construction of buildings – as airfield site

SITE No. 1

No.	SAW	A.M. No.	Con	Description
1	–	–	½H	Picket post
2–6	375	3472/42	H	Officers' quarters for 4 each
7	275	–	B	Officers' ablutions and latrines 6 lats, 6 abluts.
8–10	375	3472/42	H	Sergeants' quarters for 8 each
11	275	–	B	Sergeants' latrines, 4 lats, 3 urinals
12	275	–	B	Sergeants' and airmen's ablutions, 38 abluts.
13–18	375	3472/42	H	Barrack huts for 12 each
19	232	16329/41	B	Airmen's latrines Type 1, 5 lats, 3 urinals
20	49	9108/41	–	Fuel compound
21–33	375	3472/42	H	Barrack huts for 12 each
34–35	275	–	B	Aimen's latrines. Total 4 lats, 6 urinals
36	–	–		M.E. plinth
37–42	–	–	J	Barrack huts 30' x 15' for 18 each

78

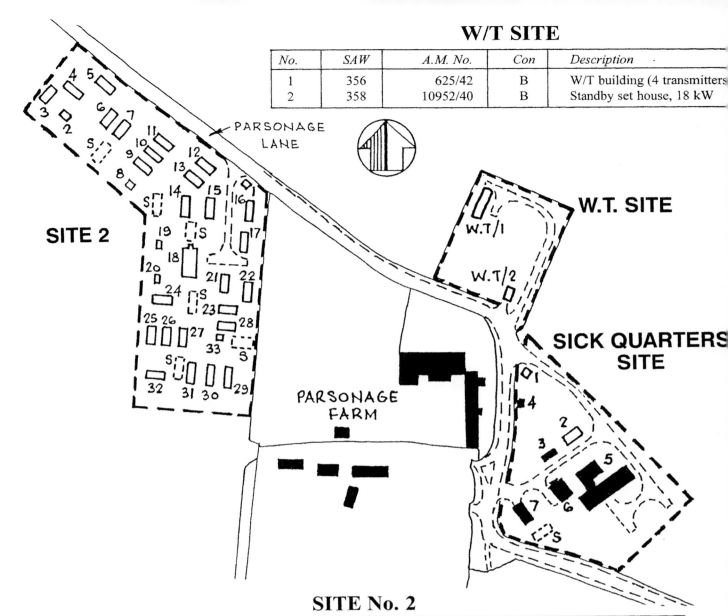

W/T SITE

No.	SAW	A.M. No.	Con	Description
1	356	625/42	B	W/T building (4 transmitters
2	358	10952/40	B	Standby set house, 18 kW

SITE No. 2

No.	SAW	A.M. No.	Con	Description
1	—	—	½H	Picket post
2	275	—	B	Officers' ablutions and latrines, 6 lats, 6 abluts.
3–7	375	3472/42	H	Officers' quarters for 4 each
8	275	—	B	Sergeants' latrines, 4 lats, 3 urinals
9–11	64	9024/41	N	Sergeants' quarters for 8 each
12–17		—	N	Barrack huts for 12 each
18	275	—	B	Sergeants' and airmen's ablutions, 38 abluts.
19–20	275	—	B	Airmen's latrines. Total 4 lats, 6 urinals.
21–32	64	9024/41	N	Barrack huts for 12 each
33	275	—	B	Airmen's latrines, 2 lats, 3 urinals.

SICK QUARTERS SITE

No.	SAW	A.M. No.	Con	Description
1	—	—	½H	Picket post
2	375	3472/42	H	Barrack hut for 12
3	65	9026/41	B	Ablutions and latrines, 2 lats, 2 urinals, 4 abluts.
4	—	—	—	M.E. plinth
5	306	2465/42	B	Sick quarters, 10 bed and dental block
6	334	3938/42	B	Sick quarters annexe, type 'B'
7	240	660/42	B	Mortuary and ambulance

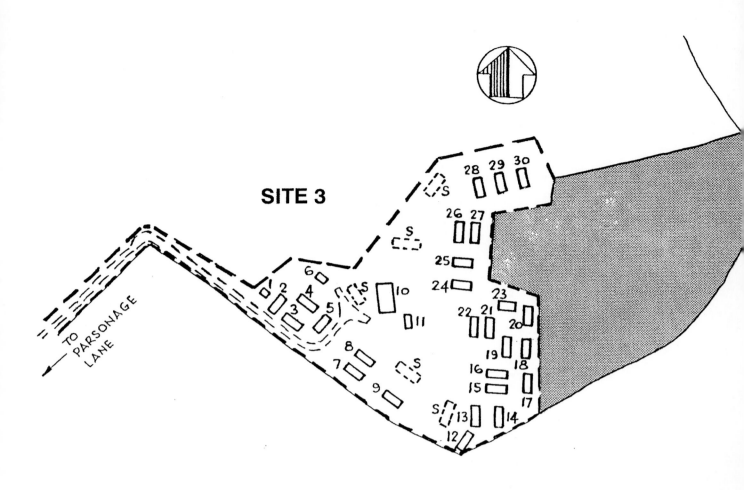

SITE 3

TO PARSONAGE LANE

SITE No. 3

No.	SAW	A.M. No.	Con	Description
1	72	12404/41	½N	Picket post
2–5	64	9024/41	N	Officers' quarters for 4 each
6	275	–	B	Officers' latrines and ablutions, 6 lats, 6 abluts.
7–9	64	9024/41	N	Sergeants' quarters for 8 each
10	275	–	B	Sergeants' and airmen's ablutions, 38 abluts
11	275	–	B	Sergeants' and airmen's latrines, 13 lats, 14 urinals
12–30	64	9024/41	N	Barrack huts for 12 each

WAAF SITE

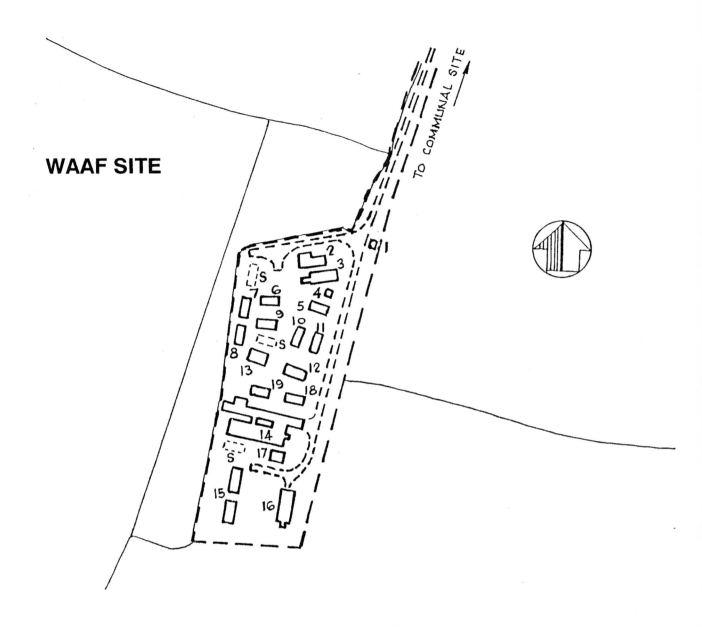

WAAF SITE

No.	SAW	A.M. No.	Con	Description
1	–	–	½H	Picket post
2	291	16333/41	B	Baths and decontamination, type 3. 5 baths, 4 showers
3	291	16333/41	B	Latrines and ablutions. 14 lats, 22 abluts
4	397	9267/42	B	Hairdressers shop, type up to 200
5–11	375	3472/42	H	Barrack huts for 12 each. Total 7 lats (1 to each hut)
12	375	3472/42	H	Sergeants' quarters for 8. 1 latrine
13	375	3472/42	H	Barrack hut for 12. 1 latrine
14	314	2454/42	B	Dining Room and institute, type 126/150
15	375	3472/42	H	Officers' mess and quarters for 4
16	284	16346/41	B	Sick quarters type 'A' (4 beds)
17	–	–	C	E.W.S. tank, open, 20,000 gal
18–19	–	–	J	Barrack huts (without lats) for 8 each

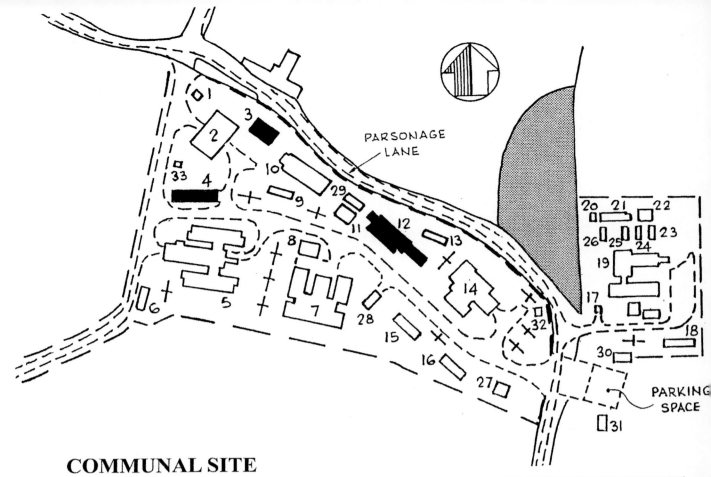

COMMUNAL SITE

No.	SAW	A.M No.	Con	Description
1	286	1580/42	B	Picket post
2	49	9108/41	–	Fuel compound, 72' x 54'
3	200	13244/41	B	Stand-by set house
4	211	14419/41	B	Grocery store, 1,000
5	344	9021/41 and	B	A/M dining room, 700 (N. wing 100' 0", S. wing 110' 0")
6	214	10107/41	B	Ration store 601/800
7	212	14395/41	B	Institute 940
8	212	14395/41	B	Institute staff quarters
9	275	–	B	A/M latrines. 27 lats, 18 urinals
10	275	–	B	Showers, ablutions and decontamination. 36 showers, 36 abluts and boiler house
11			C	E.W.S. tank, open, 20,000 gal
12	410	–	B	Gymnasium, cinema and chapel
13	275	–	B	Sergeants' baths. 12 showers, 2 basins, 3 lats, 2 urinals and boiler house
14		14436/41	B	Sergeants' mess for 84
15	287	16352/41	B	Barbers shop
16	357	5761/42	B	Education
17	286	1580/42	B	Picket post
18	224	9023/41	B	C.O's quarters
19	207	629/42	B	Officers' mess, 65
20	–	–	B	Officers' latrines. 3 lats, 3 urinals, 3 basins
21	275	–	B	Officers' baths. 9 slippers, 10 showers and boiler house
22	220	16589/40	B	Squash court, single
23–26	–	–	J	Officers' quarters, 30' x 15' for 3 each
27	402	–	B	Post office, 21' x 23'
28	–	–		Fire tender hut, 36' x 18'
29	–	–	B	WAAF latrines. 6 lats, 4 abluts.
30	–	–	N	Spare
31	–	–	½H	Spare
32	–	–	–	M.E. plinth
33	50	9559/40	B	Destructor house

APPENDIX 1

Commanding Officers of Mathams Wood ALG / RAF Sawbridgeworth

15. 6.40	Flight Lieutenant P F Edinger, (2 (AC) Sqn)
24.10.40	Wing Commander A J W Geddes, (2 (AC) Sqn)
11. 8.41	Squadron Leader D I C Eyres
23.11.41	Flight Lieutenant (later Sqn Ldr) K K Horn
15.12.42	Wing Commander Bristow
1. 6.44	Squadron Leader G Sudworth
1.12.44	Squadron Leader H F G Tristram (42 Group)
17. 4.45	Flying Officer G Partos (247 MU)

APPENDIX 2

Units at Sawbridgeworth

Unit	From	To	Main Equipment	Code Letters
39 Sqn	4.16 –	11.18	B.E.2e, B.E.12a Bristol F.2b	Not known
13 Sqn	9. 8.37 –	8. 9.37	Hawker Hector	No codes
2 Sqn	15. 6.40 –	15.10.40	B P Defiant F1 Westland Lysander 1, 2	Code KO
7th Hampshire	18. 6.40 –	23.10.40	No aircraft	
10th Essex	23.10.40 –	31. 1.42	No aircraft	
2 Sqn	24.10.40 –	19. 7.41	B P Defiant F1 Lysander 2, 3	Codes KO,XV
2 Sqn	23. 7.41 –	4. 8.41	Lysander 2, 3	Code XV
2 Sqn	10. 8.41 –	5.12.41	Curtiss Tomahawk 1, 2 Fairey Battle 1 & TT, Lysander 2 ,3	Code XV
241 Sqn	25. 8.41 –	5.12.41	Tomahawk 1, 2 Lysander 3, 3a	Code RZ
268 Sqn	25. 8.41 –	5.12.41	Tomahawk 1, 2b Lysander 2, 3	Code NM
2 Sqn	7.12.41 –	14.7.42	Tomahawk 2b, Fairey Battle 1 & TT, North American Mustang 1	Code XV
2770 RAFR	1. 2.42 –	30. 9.42	No aircraft	
16 Sqn	1. .6.42 –	3. 6.42	Mustang 1	No code
225 Sqn	1. 6.42 –	3. 6.42	Mustang 1	Code WU
613 Sqn	1. 6.42 –	3. 6.42	Mustang 1	Code SY
613 Sqn	1. 7.42 –	4. 7.42	Mustang 1	Code SY
613 Sqn	14. 7.42 –	16. 7.42	Mustang 1	Code SY
231 Sqn	11. 7.42 –	14. 7.42	Tomahawk 1, 2a	No code
268 Sqn	14. 7.42 –	26. 7.42	Mustang 1	Code NM
2 Sqn	21. 7.42 –	31. 1.43	Fairey Battle TT Mustang 1	Code XV
809 FAA	13. 9.42 –	19. 9.42	Fairey Fulmar 2	Not known
809 FAA	30. 9.42 –	11.10.42	Fairey Fulmar 2	Code '6'
239 Sqn	5.11.42		Mustang 1	Code HB
182 Sqn	7.12.42 –	17. 1.43	Hawker Typhoon 1b	Code XM
211 MU	14.12.42 –	30. 9.45	No a/c – at Hyde Hall	
182 Sqn	20 1.43 –	30. 1.43	Hawker Typhoon 1b	Code XM
3226 Servicing Commando Unit	31. 1.43 –	5. 4.43	No aircraft	
652 Sqn	20. 2.43 –	28. 3.43	Taylorcraft Auster 1, 3	No codes
268 Sqn	6. 3.43		Mustang 1a	Code NM
2 Sqn	27. 4.43 –	17. 7.43	Battle TT, Mustang 1a	Code XV

Unit	From	To	Main Equipment	Code Letters
1495 TT Flt	5.43 –10. 7.43		Hawker Henley 2 Miles Martinet 1 Lysander 2, 3, 3a	No codes
2759 RAFR	30. 6.43 – 13. 7.43		No aircraft	
410 R&SU	1. 9.43 – 30.11.43		No aircraft	
53 Mobile Field Hospital & 3 Casualty Air Evacuation Unit	23. 9.43 – 10.11.43		No aircraft	
54 MFH & 4 CAEU	26. 9.43 – 10.11.43		No aircraft	
2876 RAFR	7.10.43 – 10.11.43		No aircraft	
2809 RAFR	15.10.43 – 15.11.43		No aircraft	
63 Sqn	12.11.43 – 30.11.43		Mustang 1, 1a	No codes
168 Sqn	12.11.43 – 30.11.43		Mustang 1a	Possibly code OE
170 Sqn	12.11.43 – 15. 1.44 (disb)		Mustang 1a	No codes
4 Sqn	30.11.43 – 2. 1.44		Mustang 1, Supermarine Spitfire PR11	No codes
2 Sqn	30.11.43 – 22. 1.44		Mustang 1a	Code XV
2 Sqn	29. 2.44 – 11. 3.44		Mustang 1a	Code XV
268 Sqn	1. 3.44 – 26. 3.44		Mustang 1a	No codes
4 Sqn	4. 3.44 – 4. 4.44		DH Mosquito PR16, Mustang 1a, Spitfire PR11	No codes
2Sqn	25. 3.44 – 4. 4.44		Mustang 1a	Code XV
80 Sqn	24. 4.44 – 6. 5.44		Spitfire 9b	Code W2
126 Sqn	30. 4.44 – 22. 5.44		Spitfire 9b	Code 5J
247 Sqn	12. 4.45 – 16. 5.46		No aircraft	
247 MU	16. 5.46 – 6.47		No aircraft	

APPENDIX 3

Aircraft types at Sawbridgeworth

1916-18	B.E.2e, B.E.12a, Bristol F2b
May 1933	Avro 504N, BAC Drone, DH Dragon, DH Fox Moth, Desoutter, Fairey Fox, Miles Satyr, Monospar, Spartan Cruiser
1937	Hawker Audax
1937–38	Hawker Hector
1940–41	Boulton-Paul Defiant
1940–41	DH94 Moth Minor
1940–43	Westland Lysander 1 – 3
1940–44	DH82 Tiger Moth
1941–42	Curtiss Tomahawk 1, 2a & 2b
1941–43	Fairey Battle 1 & TT
1942	Fairey Fulmar 2
1942–43	DH84 Dominie
1942–43	Hawker Hurricane 1
1942–43	Hawker Typhoon 1b
1942–44	Airspeed Oxford
1942–44	Miles Magister
1942–44	Miles Master 2, 3
1942–44	North American Mustang 1, 1a
1942–44	Percival Proctor 2, 3
1943	Hawker Henley 2, 3
1943	Miles Martinet 1
1943	Taylorcraft Auster 1, 3
1944	DH98 Mosquito PR16
1944	Supermarine Spitfire 5c, 9, 9b, PR11
1959–73	DH82a Tiger Moth
1959–73	DHC Chipmunk Mk 23
1963–73	Hiller 360
1978–82	Piper PA22 Pawnee
1983–88	Grumman AgCat

APPENDIX 4

Representative on-base aircraft serials

Avro 504N	G-EBVY	Miles Satyr G-ABVG
DH Dragon	G-ACCR	Monospar G-ABUZ
DH Fox Moth	G-ACCF	
Spartan Cruiser	G-ABKK, 'BVY, 'BYW, VH-UQA	
Desoutter	G-AANE	(All BHAP)
Airspeed Oxford	(2 Sq)	DF234
Boulton-Paul Defiant 1	(2 Sq)	N1572
Curtiss Tomahawk	(2 Sq)	AH857, 921, (Mk 1)
		AH899, 908, 916, 934, 940, 942, 998, (Mk 2a)
		AK107, 144, 146 (Mk 2b)
DH Dominie	(2 Sq)	R5921, 9555
DH Mosquito	(4 Sq)	MM273, 276, 286, 299, 303, 309, 313 (PR16 – 'B' Flight)
	(4 Sq)	W4077 (T3 – 'B' Flight)
DH Moth Minor	(2 Sq)	X5115
DH Tiger Moth	(2 Sq)	N3904, 4954, 9304, 9325, 9454, T7329, DE358
Fairey Battle	(2 Sq)	K7683, P5288 (Mk 1), K9277 (TT conversion)
Fairey Fulmar 2	(809 Sq)	X8621, 759, DR634, 659, 715, 718, 732, 733, 738
Hawker Hector	(13 Sq)	K8096
Hawker Henley	(1495 TT Flt)	L3247
Hawker Hurricane 1	(182 Sq)	AG232
Hawker Typhoon	(182 Sq)	R7624, 629 (Mk 1a)
		R7677, 8840, 8979, DN246, 319, 422, EJ952, EK388,
		JP397, 654, 913, JR220, 427, 517, MM995, MN340,
		575, 823 (Mk 1b)
Miles Martinet 1	(1495 Flt)	HP269
Miles Master	(2 Sq)	DK882, DL876 (Mk 2)
		W8954, 8996, DL674 (Mk 3)
N A Mustang 1	(2 Sq)	AG358, 370, 401, 403, 404, 451, 456, 464, 474, 478, 488,
		492, 539, 541, 550, 551, 569, 574, 593, 605, 607, 620,
		623, 630, 633, 638, 645, AL962, 969, 972, 995,
		AM105, 112, 113, 153, 179, 183, 234, 254,
		AP164, 169, 203, 210, 220, 237, 241, 245
	(4 Sq)	AG361, 398, 426, 487, 519, 599, 664, AM127, 141, 153,
		207, 209, 223, 227, 244, AP158, 167, 213, 247, 255, 260
		('C' Flt – some loaned frequently to 2 Squadron)
	(63 Sq)	AG460, 498, 539, 575, 596, 613, AL965, AM156, 157,
		205, AP177, 196
N A Mustang 1a	(2 Sq)	FD444, 477, 480, 501, 529, 547, 552, 567
	(63 Sq)	FD445, 495, 528, 540, 561
	(168 Sq)	FD439, 444, 478, 502, 531, 565
	(170 Sq)	FD480, 483, 490, 494, 500, 502, 504, 506, 509, 536,
		543, 544, 559, 563, 566, 581, 583
	(268 Sq)	FD434, 441, 471, 486, 488, 495, 503, 535, 544, 559, 561, 563
Percival Proctor	(2 Sq)	Z7208 (Mk 2), HM354 (Mk 3)
Supermarine Spitfire	(4 Sq)	EN680, MB949, PA852, 857, 884, 887, 891, 897, 901,
		PA931, PL759, 764, 786, 787, 831, 843, 897, PM132
		(Mk PR11 – 'A' Flight)
	(80 Sq)	EE780, 839, EF680, ER471, 822, ES140, 359,
		JG875, JK145, JL164, MA828 (Mk 5c)
		EN172, BS556, JL227, MA456, 671, MH319, 880, MJ311,
		(Mk 9)
	(126 Sq)	MJ313, 623, MK211, 309, 481, 660, 893,
		ML214, NH295, 381, 406 (Mk 9b)
Taylorcraft Auster	(652 Sq)	LB322–329, 337–341, 350, 351, 374, 377 (Mk 1)
		MZ103, 104, 106, 122-125, 133, 135, 137, 139, 141,
		MZ143, 157, 158, 160, 161, 163 (Mk 3)
Westland Lysander	(2 Sq)	L4687, 692, 694, 699, 700, 702, 705, 706, 711 (Mk 1)
	(1419 Flt)	R2626 (Mk 1)
	(2 Sq)	L4780, 810, 815, 6847, 6852, N1203, 217, 226, 242, 258,

Westland Lysander (continued)	259, 262, 318, 319, P1686, 721, 9067, 070, 107, 132, 9666, 652, R9020, 9029 (Mk 2)
	T1528, 531, 532, 613, 631, 686, 696, V9287, 660 (Mk 3)
Grumman AgCat (Bowker AS)	G-BEIJ
Piper PA22 Pawnee (Bowker AS)	G-BILL, 'FPS, 'FBX

APPENDIX 5

Articles dropped, aircraft crashed or force-landed at/near Sawbridgeworth

26. 6.12	Farman type biplane (Grahame-White Aviation Co Ltd, Hendon) force-landed near 'Dusty Miller' public house, Gilston. Took off but crashed into trees, Lewis Turner uninjured.
14. 9.17	Aeroplane came down at Tednambury, close to Spellbrook CE school.
17.11.26	Gloster Grebe (29 Sqn, Duxford) force-landed at High Wych.
13. 8.37	Hector K8096 (13 Sqn). F/O B E Smith-Rewse swung on landing at Mathams Wood ALG after close recon practice and wingtip hit ground.
11. 7.40	Lysander 2 N1242 (2 Sqn). F/Lt D I C Eyres landed on ALG heavily on tail unit in gusty conditions after photo sortie
24. 7.40	Lysander 2 N1259 (2 Sqn). P/O B K Thomas made heavy landing on ALG and damage due to heavy landing made on 21.7.40 found.
20. 8.40	Lysander 2 L6847 (2 Sqn). P/O M M Lambert taxied to dispersal on ALG after refuelling but tailwheel damaged when it fell into rabbit hole.
19. 9 40	He 111P-2 G1+GL (3/KG55). Hit by AA fire and crashed at Thorley Wash, Spellbrook. Three crew killed, one wounded.
2.10.40	Lysander 2 N1319 (2 Sqn). P/O P H Watts stalled in on ALG after photo flight, tail unit damaged.
10.10.40	1000 kg bomb dropped on town by Ju88. Two adults, three children killed in Cambridge Road.
15.10.40	Lysander 2 P1686 (2 Sqn). P/O M M Lambert struck ridge landing on ALG after coastal reconnaissance
16.10.40	Ju88A-5, 4D+DM (Stab 2/KG30). Shot down by HAA from London IAZ and crashed on Much Hadham Road 1m north of ALG. Three crew plus one passenger killed.
18.10.40	Two parachute mines dropped near Gt Hyde Hall, one exploded in mid-air shattering windows at Fawbert and Barnard school, other exploded in river. No casualties.
20.10.40	Nine bombs dropped on Gt Hyde Hall cricket field. No casualties.
24.10.40	Moth Minor X5115 (2 Sqn). P/O G Grant-Govan stalled in during landing practice at new airfield and undercarriage collapsed.
27.10.40	Lysander 2 P9070 (2 Sqn). P/O D H Stuart undershot on landing at airfield and hit hedge, wire fence and bank after dawn sortie.
5. 1.41	Six bombs dropped west of town by cloud-flying Ju88s, more dropped closer to a/f later in day. No casualties.
21. 2.41	Lysander 3 T1696 (2 Sqn). F/O A E Houseman struck ground on a/f hard when landing after night-flying practice.
20. 4.41	Bombs dropped in town. Factory near SHQ set on fire.
8. 5.41	Lysander 3 R9020 (2 Sqn). F/L F M Benito swung after landing on a/f following message-drop practice and tipped on one wing when tyre burst and brakes failed.
21. 6.41	Lysander 3 R9020 (2 Sqn). Stalled in landing on a/f, u/c collapsed.
9. 9.41	Tomahawk 2a AH945 (2 Sqn). P/O H G F Larsen bounced in landing on rough a/f surface after training flight, swung and u/c collapsed.
10. 9.41	Tomahawk 2a AH928 (2 Sqn). P/O P Constant ditto.
12. 9.41	Tomahawk 2a AH927 (2 Sqn). P/O P Constant ditto.
16. 9.41	Tomahawk 2a AH940 (2 Sqn). F/Lt F M G Scotter had engine failure on take-off, landed with u/c up straight ahead.

5.10.41	Spitfire 1 R7033 (1 PRU, Benson). F/O A H W Ball blacked out when control lost in thunderstorm on combat exercise, he was thrown out and landed by parachute, aircraft broke up when starboard wing failed and crashed one mile north of a/f near Butlers Hall.
15. 4.42	Tomahawk 2a AH941 (2 Sqn). F/O C K Parkes force-landed on a/f after engine failure in circuit on test flight.
23. 4.42	Tomahawk 2b AK146 (2 Sqn). F/Lt P B Hall baled out after losing control in cloud, aircraft crashed onto searchlight battery at Gaston Green, two miles east of a/f.
9. 5.42	Mustang 1 AG401 (2 Sqn). P/O P Tonkin landed after low-flying message-drop exercise when pitot head was lost on hitting power cables near Tring, taxied at speed off edge of runway mesh and into hole. Aircraft tipped onto nose, breaking propeller.
9. 5.42	Mustangs 1 AG403 and AG488 (2 Sqn). P/O G L Gosnell in AG403 on take-off run for message-dropping practice struck AG488 taxi-ing down adjacent grass area. AG403 climbed sixty feet, stalled and crashed inverted on a/f, killing pilot. AG488 damaged, P/O P J Wilmett injured.
17. 6.42	Mustang 1 AG569 (2 Sqn). P/O M Wylie landed heavily on a/f after mail flight, tailwheel collapsed.
24. 6.42	Mustang 1 AG607 (2 Sqn). F/O W Shepherd had engine failure on take off, landed heavily straight ahead in farm field, tailwheel collapsed.
7. 7.42	Mustang 1 AG456 (2 Sqn). P/O Symonds damaged propellor due to tipping aircraft on nose whilst taxi-ing too fast after landing on a/f.
11. 8.42	Battle 1 K9277 (2 Sqn). U/c collapsed after a/c picketted on a/f.
29.10.42	Mustang 1 AG605 (2 Sqn). P/O D B Williams killed on crashing into trees near Ware trying to find a/f in bad visibility after training flight.
29.10.42	Mustang 1 AG633 (2 Sqn). P/O P W Leah crashed in farm field near a/f following landing overshoot in bad visibility after training flight.
10.11.42	Mustang 1 AM179 (2 Sqn). P/O H H J Skinner landed wheels up on a/f after local flight
22.11.42	Mustang 1 AM105 (2 Sqn). F/O J Ingham suffered total hydraulic failure on return from operations and force-landed on a/f.
25.11.42	Tomahawk 2b AK144 (2 Sqn). P/O P M Gordon-Crosby injured when engine failed during landing on a/f after local flight due to mishandling engine controls, aircraft stalled and spun in.
30.12.42	Battle 1 K9277 (2 Sqn). Tail fell off a/c due to metal fatigue when taxi-ing over rough ground on a/f. P/O P Tonkin not to blame.
16. 2.43	Typhoon 1b DN422 on delivery flight. F/Lt M J Gray aborted take-off run, throttled back and swung off runway into crash tender.
3. 4.43	P47c Thunderbolt (335FS, 4FG). 2nd Lt Smolenski killed in crash on outskirts of a/f when failing engine caught fire during landing approach.
10. 6.43	Spitfire 5b EP253 (19 Sqn). Sgt J M Ritchie force-landed west of Much Hadham after tree foliage blocked radiator on non-operational flight. Pilot slightly injured and brought to SSQ for examination.
1. 7.43	Mustang 1 AG539 (2 Sqn). F/O W Redman landed after local flight but tailwheel would not lower. Fuselage strained.
5. 7.43	Mustang 1 AP220 (2 Sqn). F/O W R Butt returned from operational flight and proceeded to beat up a/f with low rolls. Crashed during second roll and caught fire, pilot killed.
8. 7.43	Mustang 1 AM234 (2 Sqn). F/Lt W Shepherd landed on a/f second in pair after training flight, caught leader's slipstream and struck ground with wingtip.
10. 7.43	Mustang 1 AG541 (2 Sqn). F/O S J Shayle-George landed on a/f in bad visibility after operational flight, ran off runway after dropping wing and tipped on nose when u/c collapsed, breaking propeller.
24.11.43	Mustang 1a FD483 (170 Sqn). F/O H W Munro killed in crash on Much Hadham Road 1½ miles north of a/f after local test flight.
28. 1.44	Spitfire force-landed on a/f, pilot safe.
23. 3.44	Mosquito PR16 MM309 (4 Sqn). F/O M P Fellowes swung on take-off for training flight and u/c collapsed. Crew safe, a/c damage 'E'.

31. 3.44	Lancaster 2 LL683 (514 Sqn). W/O W L McGowan force-landed in field next to a/f when fuel ran low after many diversions, on returning from operational flight in bad weather conditions.
25. 6.44	V1 flying bomb fell WNW Tharbies Farm. Glass, crops and power cables damaged, no casualties.
7. 7.44	V1 flying bomb fell NE of town. Glass damaged at Hyde Hall house and lodge, no casualties.
24. 7.44	V1 flying bomb fell S of Actons Farm, High Wych, no casualties.
3. 8.44	V1 flying bomb fell on railway line near Much Hadham. 16 houses damaged, no casualties.
11. 8.44	V1 flying bomb fell on Exnells Farm. Houses damaged, no casualties.
12. 8.44	B26 Marauder 42-107611 (344 BG). Lt J D Ashford belly-landed on a/f when one engine cut on take-off from Stansted. Bombs jettisoned, injured crew treated by SSQ staff.
21. 9.44	Douglas C47 (315 TCG). Force-landed on a/f on return from airborne operation to Arnhem.
16.10.44	Airspeed Horsa (HGCU). Slipped tow on cross-country flight and force-landed on a/f with controls u/s.
9. 1.45	V2 long-range rocket (Big Ben 495) fell in field SE of town. No casualties.
11. 1.45	4000 lb RAF bomb fell in field N of Hadham Park. Glass at Hadham Park Farm and six cottages at Bury Green damaged, no casualties.
17. 1.45	V2 long-range rocket (Big Ben 555) fell in orchard at Kettle Green. 40 houses damaged, one slight casualty.

Bibliography

A Time To Fly (the memoirs of Sir Alan Cobham) Pub: Shepheard & Walwyn

'AIR 28 & 29' files at PRO, Kew

Birkenhead, Wallasey and Wirral newspaper series

Coastal, Support & Special Squadrons of the RAF (J D R Rawlings) Pub: Janes

Control Towers (Paul Francis) Pub: Airfield Research Publishing

Flight Most Secret, Air Missions for SOE & SIS (Gibb McCall) Pub: William Kimber

Great Interruption (S/L Laurence Irving) Pub: Airlife

Hertfordshire Mercury & Herts and Essex Observer newspaper series

MI9, Escape & Evasion 1939-1945 (M R D Foot & J M Langley) Pub: Book Club Assoc.

Operations Record Books for MUs 3, 211 & 247, Mobile Field Hospitals 53 & 54, RAF Regiments 2759, 2770, 2809 & 2876, & RAF squadrons 2, 4, 13, 63, 80, 126, 168, 170, 182, 231, 239, 241, 268, 613, 652 & 1495 (TT) Flt (PRO, Kew)

Second To None, the story of 2 (AC) Squadron (J G Onderwater) Pub: Airlife

The Blitz Then & Now (Vol 3) Pub: Battle of Britain Prints International

The Civil Engineer at War (Pub 1947)

The History Of The Royal Air Force Regiment (Official Publication)

This England magazine

2 (AC) Squadron Archives, RAF Marham

We landed by moonlight (Hugh Verity) Pub: Ian Allan Ltd

5090   58/36. Pt.T. 18·5·46. F10" //6400' TOPO

Overhead vertical taken post-war of the airfield site. The mesh runways are in the process of being removed, with white 'out of use' crosses painted on the concrete lead-ins at each runway end, but the rest of the site is intact. The square field at top left next to Mathams Wood is the 1937 landing ground. Blounts Farm is centre left with Allens Green village at bottom left and Shingle Hall at the bottom right.

58 Squadron/Ministry of Defence photo via RCHM

2 (AC) Sqn Tornado passenger – 1995 style. Author on scrounge duty in GR1A ZA401 'R' wears 1965 pattern boots and coverall Mk 14b over olive drab cotton Tee shirt Mk 2 and 'shreddies'. The Mk 31 life preserver has an armed personal locator beacon on the left chest with the right shin of the Mk 4 'G' trousers housing a Mk 3 knife above the 2 leg restraints for the ejection system. Tubing from the Mk 12 personal equipment connector is for the supply of high pressure air and oxygen to, respectively, the 'G' system and the Mk P12 oxygen mask, and has the radio link to the Mk 10b dark green twin-visored flying helmet. White gloves are sweat-resistant Mk 3 in fashionable Cape leather.

Total weight of kit without the full immersion and NBC suits is in the order of 35 lbs.

Aircraft AUW (with PR pack, 2 wing tanks, 2 x 1000lb GP bombs) – 61700 lbs.

Roger Brookwick photo

The Author

The author is a Structural Engineer who became interested in airfield architecture through his work. An active member of both the Airfield Research Group and Mosquito Aircraft Museum he has always been keenly interested in matters relating to aviation history and had numerous articles published on the subject.

Currently living on the edge of a former RFC/RAF fighter airfield, out of which he flew between 1966 to 1981 when it was a 'disused' site, he is reminded of the great advances in aviation made mainly during two world wars, all of which is now past but comparatively recent history.